How Your Mind WILL MAKE YOU WELL

Be Still & Know
MEDITATION

A Simple Calming Technique

ROY MASTERS

Edited by Dorothy Baker

Foreword by
Chaplain (LTC) Phillip L. Pringle

Published by The Foundation of Human Understanding
Printed in the United States of America

For information, please direct your inquiry to:
The Foundation of Human Understanding
PO Box 1000, Grants Pass, Oregon 97528, USA
Call Toll Free 1-800-877-3227. Web site: www.fhu.com
Email: books@fhu.com

Cover Design: Connie Walser Derek

Library of Congress Catalog Card No. 76-9919
ISBN 978-1466415621

Contents

FOREWORD

I am always looking for morally and psychologically sound materials that a chaplain can use to boost a unit's morale and enhance a soldier's resilience. Your [meditation] is an effective and practical tool that enhances stress management and builds resilience within the mind and emotion of the warrior.

I am especially thankful for the *Be Still & Know* exercise. It is a good self awareness exercise, comparable to the concept of mindfulness used within the field of empirically researched psychology. I have integrated the exercise into my own personal life as a Christian Chaplain. It assists me in being effective in what I call a listening prayer. My foundational written statement for listening prayer is found in Psalm 46:10, "Be still and know I am God." The essence of this spiritual discipline calms my soul, improves my emotional regulation, and enhances my critical thinking skills.

I read a small, but powerful book by Charles Swindoll, *Intimacy with the Almighty,* several years ago. This book helped transform my life as a war veteran chaplain. The book clarified if I am to be resilient in this difficult world, I must practice the four spiritual disciplines of simplicity, silence, solitude, and surrender. The *Be Still and Know* exercise helped me practice these four disciplines on a consistent basis.

My average day is filled with phone calls, emails, visits, and deadlines. It seems to me the Blackberry and computer tend to escalate distress signals in my brain as I suffer with an overload of information and tasks to be completed each day. Charles Swindoll said it best when he stated, "Everything around us works against reordering and simplifying our lives. Everything! Ours is a complicated and cluttered world." The *Be Still & Know* exercise used as a listening prayer decreases the clutter in my mind and helps me be more effective and creative in my thought process.

The practice of silence and solitude is at the very core of the *Be Still & Know* exercise. Learning to be still is one of the most needed, yet most difficult spiritual disciplines today. I remember my struggle when I first became intentional about practicing being still. It was just like the noted Roman Catholic Priest, Henri Nouwen stated, "Time in solitude may at first seem little more than a time in which we are bombarded by thousands of thoughts and feelings that emerge from hidden areas of our mind. It can feel like a multitude of confusing thoughts are jumping around in the mind like monkeys in a banana tree." Indeed, this was my experience early on. However, I have observed as I continue the practice of silence and solitude my mind becomes more rested. It also seems my resilience in thinking straight under pressure is improved.

Last of all, there is the issue of surrender. It is an issue of how I want my day to go versus how my day actually does go.

A few years ago, while practicing the essence of be still and know, I came to a powerful awareness of what my core daily struggle is. I want my day to go my way. I am finally learning to let go of those things I cannot control or change. I am finally learning that surrendering my days and future to God, not as I would have it, is the most responsible act of obedience I can do. This transformative attitude is a lighter burden for me to carry. It certainly decreases my frustration and distress levels.

I need simplicity, silence, solitude, and surrender in my life to be an effective, resilient military chaplain in today's complex world. Thank you for introducing me to the *Be Still & Know* CD. It is a helpful tool that can help many other military personnel become the resilient leaders we all need to be in the rapidly changing environment in which we live.

Chaplain (LTC) Phillip L. Pringle
US Army (Southern Baptist)

INTRODUCTION

This book is about a very special form of meditation—a rediscovery of an ancient science that provides the answer to the serious problems of our time. Proper understanding of this technique is apparent only after you have submitted yourself to its discipline for a time. How short or how long a time, the author cannot predict. To some, enlightenment comes with sudden intensity. To others it is a gradual unfolding.

What follows is divided into two parts. One part is for conscious reading or listening, in order to bear witness to what you will discover. The other, more vital part is the meditation itself, a process that will raise your conscious self, now dangerously absorbed into its thinking, to the surface of the mind, a place where pure understanding about your problems exists. You simply cannot understand or resolve your problems from the point of being involved with them. Trying to do so causes things to go from bad to worse.

The meditation exercise will also show you how to overcome certain reactions to stress. Through meditation, you will begin to see that all your troubles come from (1) doubting the truth, (2) being ambitious and (3) living out of the emotional upset which results from and perpetuates the first two mistakes. Your failure attempts to deal with *symptoms* and in compensating for your guilt have only made matters worse.

The meditation will help you realize that any attempt to rationalize or analyze an emotional complex only adds to the severity of the problem. The author is well aware of the controversial nature of these statements and politely requests the reader to withhold judgment until some experience with the meditation is gained.

Most people rebel at "good" advice that opposes their secret ambitions, and they will recoil when you talk about their faults. Alcoholics will rebel when you criticize their drinking, even when you try to help them. We all abhor outer direction (being told what to do), for the natural inclination of the soul is toward ultimate *self-government*.

For example, fixed on the wall of an elevator there is a sign: "Gentlemen, please remove your hats when ladies are present." The first man to see it becomes angry; the sign is insinuating that he has no manners, so he rebels by leaving his hat on. A second man enters and becomes self-conscious, noticing that the ladies also see the sign. Reluctantly, he removes his hat.

The first man might have had good manners, but when he saw the sign he rebelled with bad manners (which bothers his conscience). The second man removed his hat only through embarrassment, not because he really wanted to, and so felt thoroughly uncomfortable all the time he was in the elevator.

Notice that both men have reacted badly to the sign. Both men lost control, as well as respect for themselves and the ladies in the elevator. Neither of these men did the right thing, and this outcome was the secret intention of the "do-gooder" who placed the notice. Now, the one who would have been right is wrong, and the unmannered person is the one who appears to be well mannered. Moreover, the meddling problem-solver has not solved the problem, but only made things worse. The frustration caused by his interference creates a greater need for his services and provides him with an inspiring illusion of worthiness. In the process, he has created a full-time job away from looking at his own miserable self.

Counseling places the same barrier between patient and healer. You simply cannot help a person from the outside. Searching people become worse off, and weak characters only seem to get better, while the doctor promotes in himself artificial feelings of value.

The smallest child will rebel against such signs as the one we mentioned above. This rebellion is the cause of many emotional diseases, compulsions, juvenile delinquency and crime. Without the kind of self-government, which is guided by conscience, the more we try to rule ourselves or instruct those we love, the more rebellion we create.

A free nation can remain free only as long as its people find the way to self-discipline. If they fail in this, socially necessary disciplines must be imposed upon them by law. That is precisely why we evolve the need for authorities: to protect us from one another because of what we have become as a result of our failure to live out of the stimulation from the principle within us.

Alas, the more laws and regulations we create, the more we lose the real freedom to live out of ourselves. There evolve so many laws covering so many things that we are left with almost no choice in anything. Thus the law must take away from us the very freedom it was supposed to protect.

Of course we need law and order, but only because we have not found them within. Would you believe that there is an unconscious wish on the part of most authorities to keep you from being lawful, healthy, self-led and motivated? The way law punishes crime does as much to create the criminal as temptation does. And medicine sets a person up to be more sick in making him well.

What we are dealing with, then, is a gigantic psychic conspiracy to make you dependent on being led! Leaders have a terrible need to be needed, and to feed their egos, people must be changed into cripples.

Failure to find the inner way means that we become enslaved to our rationale and our lawless passions, so that eventually they have to be held in check for us by pills and jails. When our feelings are forcibly controlled or manipulated from the outside by the very rules we should have chosen for ourselves from the inside, we live in angry agony. We must learn to lead our own feelings and bodies. We must also discover how to let others find this way for themselves.

The soul of man stands in the middle of two worlds: the material and the spiritual. The one to which we respond controls us. Our path of existence depends on our choice in this matter. By not choosing rightly, or not knowing how, we continue responding to a compulsive external tug on our senses which causes us the agony of rebelling against or conforming to what only *appears* to be right.

Pavlov demonstrated that dogs would respond increasingly to repeated stimuli with "idea" and feeling, and eventually "idea" alone could produce the reaction. Conditioned reflex may be normal for animals, but it spells agony for mankind, daily robbing him of the will to do right.

In the outwardly motivated person, ideas rise out of reaction to things or people or situations. These ideas grow to create feelings (usually of fear) through the continued "idea-feeling" relationship in much the same manner as Pavlov's dogs. They were conditioned to salivate at the ring of a bell by having food present. When the food was removed, the idea of food associated with the bell was sufficient to cause the same reaction. Similarly, man has guilt or panic buttons that can be pressed for another's advantage, because his reason has not been developed as a stronger influence than outside pressures.

Every person who allows the undisciplined emotional reaction to temptation is guilty, afraid and easily controlled by those growing sensitivities. Emotional response motivates behavior patterns as the result of external pressures, creating a vicious cycle of feeling and thinking that bypasses reason. This, then, is the cause of all our suffering. (As a matter of record here, man no longer has any reason, it having been displaced by excuses and rationale to hide the shame of his enslavement to corrupting influences.)

The meditation is the science of starting a similar stimulation from the other side of the psyche. It is a science of diminishing response to temptation, persons or things. By eliminating the response to outer stimulation, we starve the roots of unfounded fears and dissolve the faulty imagination, opening up a whole new world of understanding. Then, and only then, do we begin to see reality.

The secret lies in the meditation exercise, a reverse principle to the hypnosis of life. All of us have within a potential inclination toward right action, such as helping one another. The exercise fosters this tendency to think and do what we perceive is wise for each moment in a naturally compelled manner, without the use of any pressure or suggestion to that end. The emphasis is placed solely upon improvement of the meditation exercise. The directions are designed to lead us to the ability to perceive clearly for ourselves and to have confidence in and act upon what we see to say and do; and so by not doubting, we can overcome the emotionality we feel when we do doubt ourselves.

America is gobbling up "success," "get rich" and "influence others" books at a tremendous rate. But are material possessions the real object of our search? The novelty of riches soon wears thin, as any child who has had a new toy can tell you. Without real purpose, our hunger and dissatisfaction grow worse than before. For unhappy people, money is a means of self-destruction. They use it to hurt others, or gamble it away on "wine, women and song" in a frantic attempt to ease the pain of externally reactive living. Having lost the joy of meeting each moment calmly, patiently, graciously, confidently, they seek the substitute reward called pleasure.

The writer does not guarantee the seeker wealth, but rather he offers knowledge of the way to contentment, peace of mind, and purpose. The road to riches is not the road to real happiness. *The road which leads to correct response in each moment of truth is the first step to everything worthwhile.*

If you were to ask ten people this question, "What would you ask for if you were granted only one wish?" the answers would vary. One might say "a new car", another might say "education," another "health," another "money"; ironically, these people would ambitiously and blindly limit their opportunities in life. If we were truly inclined toward Reality, we might choose quite differently. We might say, "If I had one wish, I would wish that every good thing I ever wished for would come true." Here we would be using this one wish to become a foundation for all other wishes. We all have that choice in life, but we cannot make that wish because it is hidden from us.

When Solomon was asked what single wish he would be granted, he answered: "Give me wisdom that I might judge Thy people properly." Because of his propensity toward good, his prayer was heard. The Lord was obliged to give Solomon riches, fame, honor, everything, because Solomon had asked for the *cause* of all good things.

We all know how beneficial wisdom and perhaps positive thinking are for us, but no one as yet has shown us how we may achieve them without kidding ourselves. A sort of pseudo-positive thinking ends when we close an inspiring book, or perhaps it lingers for a while after we listen to a lecture. So we spend more and more time on drinking in good thoughts, which are all too soon washed out by one good emotional upset. Conversely, the truly positive state of mind effortlessly influences conditions, and adversity builds its strength.

The salesman cannot close a sale if he reacts to his customer; the customer must respond to the salesman. If you go through life being influenced by others, you cannot be positive. True positiveness is the effect on life that comes about simply through not being affected by it. This beautiful thing comes to pass by discovering a relationship with our Parent Self. If we let the Presence within affect us more than our environment, we remain calm—less and less affected by stress. Because we lack this alignment, most of us react negatively to pressure. Because of this compulsion to respond, we spend so much time finding ways to relax and release guilt, worrying about how to overcome life and analyzing everything, that it drains us of the energy we need for successful living. Our tense minds become so clouded we cannot concentrate, and we make so many foolish decisions that we are afraid to face life. A positive state of mind comes about only when we are no longer affected by such confusions.

Doctors agree that many diseases stem from needless reaction to stress. It has been fairly well established that emotion brings about abnormal changes in the body, changes that lead to illness. Tense people may become sick because of reaction, and then worry themselves into more illness.

The smoker, the alcoholic and the compulsive eater all worry about their problem, but the more they think about it the more they feed the problem. The more they try to abandon their habits, the more they are reminded of a growing unsoothed agony of tension. The harder they try to overcome it, the more strongly it resists their efforts. This is an example of the law of reversed effort, found in all man's personal problems. What we fight we give power to evolve, so that through our struggle we compound the problem we are fighting, the very problem that we ourselves originated. Nothing can live without its sustaining factor. This is true also of sickness and disease—when we remove the foundation of pride and struggle, our problems wither away.

We stampede headlong into the arms of comfort and complacency to escape the pains of stress, never realizing that these conditions, properly handled, are the sole pathway to health. Ironically, the security, the soft living we pursue (to avoid experience), eventually becomes the cause of further suffering. We must, like Solomon, seek the basic wisdom to cope with our problems and then we must again face life armed with patience and self-control.

In learning to play the piano, one must have a piano to practice on. If one has learned incorrectly, one cannot overcome the errors of past learning without a piano on which to practice in a new way. It is the same with life. Take the case where one person reacts to trifles while another remains unaffected. Both of these persons have had experience (the equivalent of practice) that has cumulatively affected their total personalities. One has emerged bitter and resentful, the other kind and strong.

As a result of each reaction, it takes less provocation to produce more reaction—eventually we have a conditioned reflex. "A" grows more sour. "B" grows stronger. "A" worries over his feelings. "B" has no guilt feelings to worry about and possesses a mind free to pursue more worthwhile interests. "A" becomes negative through his reactions to stress. The only way "A" can improve is to imitate "B"; but without both the understanding and the living experience, "A" cannot start changing (like the man who cannot relearn the piano without a piano and new instructions).

The situation that causes the problem in "A" is also the identical situation by which he can recover. Suppose "A" is irritated by his mother-in-law—every time he sees her she makes him more nervous. Let us assume that his reaction (resentment) is producing the problem. If we teach him how to overcome his reaction to his mother-in-law, he recovers—and can extend his new-found patience into his relations with other people. Failure to accomplish this can lead to diminishing control, increased tension, resentment and bitterness.

As we lose control of ourselves, it takes less stress to produce more reaction. Eventually, a complete loss of self-control leads to a shock or sickness, which kills us. We must learn to reverse this state of affairs so that it will take more stress to produce less reaction. If we go along in the old way, we lose our ability to face the smaller issues of life, but if we learn the new way of meeting life, we grow more adept as greater challenges arise.

Our Creator has given us an inner conditioning process to override our animal responses under stress. Through meditation we can pattern our responses from the soil of inner reason, for the secret of controlling "things" lies in the proper response to the intuitive self. The dissolving of our animal feelings of need and hate will mark the beginning of our divine love for others.

Inner conflict exists only because we lack proper understanding of this exact science. At present, we are controlled by feeling, and feeling is directed by evil pressures, both those that hypnotize us to be bad and those that try to make us feel good. People and things have made us puppets. Response to environment causes a conflict, which we tend to relieve through pleasure that gives us more pain simply because it is wrong conditioning, a wrong way of solving a problem. The study of this response pattern is the basis of modern psychology, but, alas for this art, it cannot change the man unless it changes the situation—and what kind of man is it who is good only when conditions are?

Why not teach the inner man to remain unmoved by the conditions surrounding him? When we respond to our environment, we take on the nature of the world we live in; when things are nice, we feel nice; when things are unpleasant or we are persecuted, we become cruel or depressed. We conform to avoid pain or to gain safety and approval, slowly giving up inner principle as we capitulate to the cruel world. When we conform, we become like others, forfeiting the privileges of creative individuality; we become addicted to seeking the pleasing effects of conditions, and that sets us up to be more affected by the next negative emotional impact. The pressure-motivated person is in conflict with his true self. The inner-motivated man is happily not bothered by his variance with others.

xviii

Here, then, is the age-old practice of meditation brought up-to-date, redefined as an exact science of developing the individual. Let me warn the traveler who is about to enter this dimension: you cannot gain any experience from reading this book. The meditation is basically a technique of subjection to the inner self, which we know as conscience. The understanding gained from entering into it is so profound that you will never find words to explain it to others. The effect of this inner attentiveness will change your perspective on life so radically and rapidly that within a very few days many people will be astonished at your new attitudes and insight.

At this point it should be mentioned that Chapter 1 of this book, "Be Still & Know," is a more or less verbatim transcription of the author's recordings of the same name. It is the key exercise in meditation, probably the only one needed by the sincere seeker. It is the author's belief that most people would prefer to learn the technique of meditation from the recordings in the privacy of their own homes. If that is the case, you may obtain the CDs from The Foundation of Human Understanding, P.O. Box 1000, Grants Pass, Oregon 97528.

The special exercise in objectivity introduces into us those true principles from the very source, not from intellectual rote. Many people know their faults, yet cannot change them; life like this is a nightmare of struggle. But when the "dreamer" separates from the nightmare of his thinking, he enters into the dimension of reality. When you are awakened from the nightmare, there is no need to struggle. Life becomes effortless. The birds sing sweeter; the sun shines brighter. Habits will melt like ice in the summer sun; you will see life from an entirely new frame of reference. You will be detached, free, as though you were the director of the play, not the puppet actor. You will experience a strong sense of awareness and control, a feeling that life is just beginning for you, a feeling of being different from the rest of the world—because you are,

If you are a scientific investigator, my advice to you is not to try this at all; your soul cannot bear to be still, for in that stillness you would feel that you were dying. (There is, of course, a "dying to the world" that is welcome to the pure in heart, but it is an anathema to the vain egotist who prides himself on the power of his intellect.)

The truth is that in order to see reality your ego must come out from hiding in its imagination to face it. You must abandon the refuge of your Alice-in-Wonderland world of imagination where you think you are something when you are not. You must look at all the compulsive cunning, analyzing, intrigue, scheming and planning to get what you want out of life which pass for intelligence. This you may not want to do, for when one sees truly in the light of reality, one experiences the shame that takes away pride, and as a proud person, that is something you will want to avoid like the plague. This experience transcends human expression. The soul, once quieted, stripped of its rationale, illicit desires, and compulsive mind-movement, comes face to face with the truth about its pride and weakness.

If you are merely curious, just read this book as long as it holds your interest (it embodies some ideas you have heard before); then put it among the other inspirational books that never did you any real, lasting good but look nice on your bookshelves. If, on the other hand, you long to see reality again, you may find in Chapter 1, "Be Still & Know," all that you need to know to start on your own journey within.

YES, 3/2/12 THIS HAPPENED FOR ME

1

Be Still & Know

I. THE PREPARATION

You are about to take a journey. It will be the most wonderful experience of your life. The secret is not apparent to the casual reader. It reveals itself only to the person who is willing to follow the step-by-step instructions and will follow through with the mental exercise by himself in the days that follow.

Do not expect a miracle instantly. Results can appear quite soon, but because of individual differences, it may be a few days, a few weeks, sometimes much longer.

Be sure that you do not do this exercise for the purpose of feeling better or to get something out of it. That attitude destroys the effectiveness of the meditation and gives it a selfish twist. Do it to discover your true self rather than to feel better. Expecting some special effect ruins the spirit of discovery and can create illusion and frustration.

For the time being, put aside your fears, anxieties, guilts and worries, and give all your attention to understanding the author's instructions to you. Repeat the meditation exercise by yourself many times a day, at least three if possible, especially first thing in the morning and last thing at night.

Careful: do not try to analyze why it works. There is a vast difference between concern and worry, analysis and understanding.

If you listen very carefully and do as you are told, you will experience periods of well-being and then periods of doubt, thoughts such as "Will it last?" or "Am I kidding myself?" Take advantage of your increased awareness to observe this out of your thinking. Be attentive in this special way and you will come to understand many things effortlessly. Analysis always substitutes for understanding and leads to worry and doubt, and doubt in turn will lead to confusion, emotion, depression and despair.

Although you cannot make yourself believe, you can observe the demon of doubt out of existence. You will see what is meant by this as you meditate.

Do not wait until you feel like doing your exercise; do it religiously. The object of the exercise, you see, is to *lead* the way you feel. Our feelings have subtle ways of talking to us and blocking us from doing what is wise. Therefore, if there is only one thing you must make yourself do, let it be to meditate. Once you have gotten past the mysterious reluctance and the resistance, you will be glad you did.

Be careful the exercise does not become a mechanical thing. Do it each time as if it were the very *first* time, so that it remains an observation exercise. There may be an uplifting, perhaps a "distant" feeling, lasting several days. As you become accustomed to this, you may start to worry, "Is it wearing off? I'm not getting anything out of my exercise. Am I doing it right?" *The distant feeling is the awareness you have been seeking all of your life.*

Most of us are accustomed to thinking from our feelings and being lost in them. We are used to living in a daydream state of escape. Continue with your exercise *regardless* of what happens. If you encounter an odd experience, *don't worry*. Wonder, watch, observe, question, wait, and you will be safe. For goodness' sake, don't decide whether it is a good experience or a bad one. It is perfectly all right if you admit that you don't know and begin to *wonder;* that's how you will come to understand.

Never add any technique to what you have been taught. The meditation exercise is what the name implies. The exercise will make the subconscious subject to the conscious understanding.

Although the instructions seem to contain many suggestions, close examination will reveal but one principle.

Never (through lack of understanding) misuse the power you develop, giving suggestions to yourself such as "I will be brave," "I will lose weight." Don't roll up your sleeves to deal with problems as you begin to understand what they are. Wait. Be patient. There is a time and place for everything that is to be said or done. The most important thing for you to experience is repentance, which is the sad gladness that is known when you see yourself in the light and you see your ego as part of the problem.

The meditation exercise contains all the ingredients for perfect self-control. The values accumulate only when practiced daily. If you want to break a habit or solve a problem, at this moment stop trying. I know it is very important to you, but up to now you have not succeeded your way, with all that effort. Put the same attention into your meditation exercise, and you will find that problems will resolve themselves. In a very short while habits will give you up, beginning with the last to appear.

There will come a time when serious guilt problems lose their place of importance. This may be quite puzzling, but remember what I said, "Do not analyze it." Just be grateful that it is so. Be patient; in time you will understand what is happening.

These words are to be your guide for a little while. Go through the basic exercise without help whenever you can. It is essential that sooner or later you learn to do it by yourself without any help from this recording or text.

The day you stop meditating will be the day you begin to fall back, *and it may be impossible to begin again, ever.*

Examine the following text and thoroughly familiarize yourself with the simple requirement of the meditation exercise technique. When you have grasped the basic concept, which is *to learn how to become objective to your own thought stream and not fall into your thoughts,* it's time to put it into practice.

You should not encounter any difficulty, but if you run into emotional blocks toward the printed word, you should obtain the instruction as it first appeared, as a sound recording in the author's voice.

You will notice that the exercise in learning objectivity phases into a discussion of basic principles. In the original classic sound recording from which this text is taken, this format was used because once the conscious mind is separated from the confusion, the education, and the prejudices of the lower subconscious self, it becomes capable of deeper understanding and of following sound principles as never before.

To be patient and calm is good advice that few can follow, except perhaps artificially by taking pills. Only in the truly objective state can the conscious mind inherit faith and, through faith, patience, and fully appreciate (and marvel at) how far the principle of patience can go. Now that the meditation is in printed form, the exercise has been separated from the principles explained by the narrator. You will note the point of separation following the end of the exercise. The author wishes to emphasize that the spoken word is far easier to follow than the written word, and he again suggests that you write for his meditation recordings if you have any difficulty.

The procedure is modified as follows: first accomplish the objective of the meditation exercise and when you have reached this objective state (which feels mildly distant), then read the principles that protect the meditative state.

This simple exercise leads your consciousness up through layers of conscious thinking while the spoken part of the dialogue shows you how to preserve this state and helps awaken you progressively to even higher realms of understanding.

II. THE MEDITATION EXERCISE

Sitting in a straight-back chair, place both feet on the floor. Close your eyes. Choose either hand and let it hang loosely by your side. Be careful not to go to sleep or to do the exercise for relaxation. The procedure is only to prevent an accumulation of tension by correctly meeting life's experiences, not to dull the effects that will follow your failure to do so.

Bring your attention to your right hand hanging by your side. Simply notice it. Feel the blood flowing down into it. It will tingle. Now just do that. Just be aware of your hand hanging by your side. *There is no need for any effort.* Again, simply notice your hand hanging by your side until you find yourself *not* noticing it through being caught up in a day-dream. When that happens, simply bring your attention back to your hand again, and again. If you will do this, you will begin to feel the blood flowing down into your fingertips. You are now learning how to concentrate on your hand. Be very, very conscious of your hand.

Mentally shift your attention from one finger to another. Shift your attention to the first finger, the second finger, the third and fourth, coming back to the first again. Just be very, very aware of each finger in turn until it begins to feel as though the blood were flowing down into it.

Now, while you are being very, very aware of your hand, at the same time (and you find you can do it) become also aware of the middle of your forehead. Now, as though you were looking through the middle of your forehead, funnel your attention down your arm into your hand.

When you notice that your mind wanders off, simply notice your hand again. Feel the awareness of your hand. Feel the hand tingling as though the blood were flowing down into it and see if you can see the outline of your hand in your mind's eye—*as though* you were peeking out of your mind's eye through the middle of your forehead. Be aware of your hand as though you were seeing it with your mind's eye through the middle of your forehead.

Keep doing this; don't stop. Be very, very aware of this hand. Be very conscious of it. Feel the presence of it. Feel the blood flowing down into it, and then out of this mild, tingling, warm feeling, let that hand become a vague outline in your mind's eye. It is as though you can almost see or sense where your hand is *without* imagery.

Now watch the thought that tries to pull you away from being aware of your hand. If your thoughts pull your awareness away from the *present* moment, bring your attention back to your hand, and then again feel the awareness of it; feel the presence of it, and then see the back of your hand drawing up toward you, so that the back of your hand comes up to touch the middle of your forehead. Draw your hand toward you as you look out at it with your mind's eye.

Be very conscious of your own mind, as though you were sitting in a big cave, and then feel the awareness of your hand and see the outline of your hand moving toward your head and your head toward your hand. Note: it is not important if such concentration does not make your arm feel light. I only want to help you to keep your mind in the now—to keep it from wandering into thought and dream stuff.

If your thoughts pull your awareness away from the tingling of your hand in this present moment, simply feel the awareness of your hand again, and then "see" your hand drawing upward toward your head and your head toward your hand. Keep doing it; don't stop.

Again, so as to help keep your awareness in the moment, judge the distance between the hand and your forehead. See if you can estimate the distance your hand has to travel to touch your forehead. Do not hurry. Be patient. You have plenty of time. Just be conscious of the tingling hand. Feel the awareness of it. See the outline of it through your mind's eye, coming toward you (as though you were looking out through the middle of your forehead), drawing closer and closer and closer. Keep doing it. (You're not meant to look up and strain your eyes.)

If your thoughts wander off, bring your mind back to the now awareness of your hand. Feel the blood flowing down into it. Feel the presence of it, and then see the outline of your hand drawing toward the middle of your forehead, as though you were looking out into space and you see it coming toward you. *But don't look upward or strain your eyes.* Simply have the awareness of the middle of your forehead, of your mind's eye. Just observe AS THOUGH you were looking through the middle of your forehead, the place where thoughts arise, and then see if you can locate where your hand is rising up toward the middle of your forehead. See if you can draw your arm up toward the middle of your forehead, energizing your arm through being very aware of it.

Do not hurry. *It is really not important if your hand does not rise.* The object of the exercise is to create in you a response to your inner self, to remain in the present, in the Presence. If your arm becomes light and buoyant, just let your hand go up by itself toward your forehead.

If your mind wanders off, bring your attention back to your hand; feel the awareness of it again. Feel the tingling sensation as if the blood were flowing down into your fingers. See the outline of your hand coming toward the middle of your forehead as though you were looking through your mind's eye. Do not strain your eyes. Just be very, very aware

of your hand as though you could see it, through the awareness of the middle of your forehead, so your hand and head
touch and feel as one.

You find now that you can dissolve unnecessary, unwanted
thoughts simply by becoming very aware of the present moment. Just be aware of your hand. Feel it coming up toward
you so that the back of your hand touches your forehead.
Judge the distance. In your estimation, see if you can judge
the distance between the back of your hand and the middle of
your forehead. Draw the hand closer to the head. Soon you
will feel that the back of your hand is closer to your forehead
than it really is. You may think to yourself, "If I move it just a
little closer, the back of my hand will touch the middle of my
forehead," but it doesn't. It may feel as though your hand is
passing through your head, rather than to your head.

But when it does move a little closer, it doesn't seem to
touch your forehead. It seems as though your hand is closer
than it really is. This is just an effect created by the way you
are concentrating.

Now still keep being aware of this hand. Be very, very
conscious of it. Feel as if the blood were flowing into it. It will
tingle. It may begin to feel warm or detached, but just keep
being aware of your hand and remain aware of it through the
middle of your forehead.

When the back of your hand touches the middle of your
forehead, drop your hand to your lap. When you have done it
with one hand, do it also with the other.

Now, while you are listening to or reading these principles, keep noticing the place in the middle of your forehead and your hand as if they were one place, joined together, or just be very conscious of your hand on your lap or by your side.

III. PRINCIPLES THAT PROTECT THE MEDITATIVE STATE

Each time you do this exercise, you are creating an increased ability to observe and thereby control your thoughts from within yourself—not because you are told to, but because the exercise makes it so. Each time you do this exercise, you will create a greater awareness of the present; and the unpleasant events of the past become less and less important—dissolved in the light of reality—not because you are told to, but because the exercise makes it so.

You should not dwell morbidly on the past or worry about the future. Wait until the reason for your problem surfaces, and when it does, notice any resentment against being shown.

Your exercise will help you to keep your awareness in the present—not because you're told to, but because the exercise makes it so. The exercise will clear your mind and cause you to realize simple principles that will be revealed to you in the place in your mind where resentment, judgment and worry arise.

Be aware of your silly ego-needs and then realize that no one can fulfill them. Be aware of the folly of looking outside to others for fulfillment. Look at your impatience, and in realizing your need for patience, patience will come. See what causes frustration and impatience. Surely it is some form of ambition for yourself or for someone. Realize the folly of that ambition.

Now, having more compassion, you need not let things upset or frustrate you, not in the slightest degree, especially those little unkind, unfair and dishonest things that people say and do to you to motivate and downgrade your ego to raise theirs.

You really ought not be annoyed inwardly or outwardly, not that you must suppress your anger. Observe your impatience, which you used as a means of getting ego-drive energy and for judging others. See the need to overlook and make allowances right at the moment, not because you have to, but because you want to.

Don't be afraid to speak up (patiently) and don't be surprised to see a lot of past suppressed resentment bubbling to the surface for release after that.

You will soon realize it is your own resentment that hurts you more than the unthinking cruelties of other people. Therefore, from now on, watch out for the opportunity to overlook and be outspoken, right on the spot—not two seconds later, but immediately, when it happens—so that you will respond more to what you know and come to know is right and less and less to conditions and people.

Learn to make allowances for everyone from now on, no

11

matter who it is—especially those who are close to you. Because you cannot control your faults (those you can see and those you cannot), it is not wise to be resentful toward the faults of others, especially your family. The ones to make allowances for first are the ones close to you; if you cannot do it for them, how can you expect to do it for strangers? On the other hand, if you are patient with them, it will be easier to cope with the pressures of the world.

True love does not expect anything from anyone. It is what you expect (ambition and ulterior motive) and do not receive that makes you frustrated and resentful. It does not matter what others have or do. When you do something for someone, do it because you see it is wise, not because you feel you have to.

You must no longer have imaginary conversations with people as to what you are going to say to so-and-so the next time you see him. Have faith. Be spontaneous.

Never mind what you should have done or could have said; what has been cannot be changed, no matter how much you wish it; but you can change from now on through having patience rather than resentment.

If you have felt disturbed about some worry or mistake in the past, remember that the people you wronged, if they were good, would have forgiven you without your asking, and if they are not good, just start making allowances from now on anyway. For it is written, "Forgive us as we forgive." This implies that each time we are patient with another, we obtain the forgiveness and salvation of God, and we undo some of our former sins.

The coward is a coward from the time he should have been brave until the next time. If he again fails to be brave, he is a greater coward with more remorse than before; but if he chooses to be courageous, he will no longer be a coward. If the world should suddenly become perfect, the coward would never have the chance to redeem himself.

So it is with you; you have allowed yourself to become judgmental and resentful over many trivial things in your life, and when you could have overlooked or made allowances, you judged. Therefore, be glad when people are rude or unkind, for here is your opportunity to be patient and so through patience give up judgment.

If there were no danger, you could not possess courage. If there were no hate or temptation, how could you develop love and virtue? Cruel and unthinking people are giving you the opportunity to accomplish now what you failed to do before. The situations that once made you upset, guilty and afraid will become the very things to give you happiness and well-being from now on.

Therefore, whosoever shall try to anger you or upset you is actually giving you the opportunity to rise above your problems. They do not know this, but they are doing you a great service, and the harder people try to upset you, the calmer you will become, the brighter you will shine. So remember to overlook right on the spot—and be plain-spoken, with firmness, kindness and patience from now on.

Whoever tries to annoy you intentionally or otherwise is trying to hurt and even control you with your own resentment. Simply observe him. Respond only with patience and whatever thought or deed that comes forth out of that center of calmness. Take resentment out of everything so that you discern, rather than judge.

Let this run through your thoughts often. Have the awareness of it in your mind at all times. Keep this as a spiritual and moral goal. Let it be more important than any material goal in this world, for it is the means by which everything can be accomplished.

Let the whole procedure of meditation give you a satisfaction and a joy of doing that will far exceed the pleasure from material things. It should be a joy to think about it, to understand it and do it again and again, so the Light will modify everything that passes through your mind from the world. —JESUS CHRIST

You should make decisions according to it. Everything you feel, do or say should conform to it; that is, to be patient, overlook on the spot and be outspoken with firmness, kindness and patience.

Meditate because you can see it is right to do, not because you have to. Do it because you yearn for understanding. Do it for the sake of finding and being committed to what is true and good; do it for the pure love of seeing truth prevail—to be a better person, regardless of profit or loss or whether or not it makes you feel good.

If you want to have a real goal to think about, let it be, "If I could just be unmoving in my patience and discern people as they are without judging them for what they do or imply,

14

I would be better off." This is the truth: no other goal will give you satisfaction, so there is no point in thinking about it. Everything here merely points to the simple instruction to overlook on the spot and be plain-spoken with firmness, kindness and patience.

♡ Part of this guidance is to help you understand. The other part is directing you to your center of dignity, to the objective state where light, patience and true love are.

- Do your exercise, and it will bring you to the inner life.

- Now, if you have something to say, say it.

- If you have something to do, do it.

- Don't be upset; say it.

- Don't be upset; do it.

As long as you are calm and patient and not upset, you cannot possibly hurt anyone with your words or deeds, and you have the right to speak up. You cannot please everyone anyway, so stop trying. You are responsible only for expressing the truth for each moment. If others become upset over your honesty, then they will see their own faults in the light of your patient nature.

The first thing, then, is to overlook—stand firm—don't react. Be patient under trial. As long as you are not resentful and judgmental, you will always be able to disagree without being disagreeable. If people are upset because of your honesty, they are not your friends anyway, and you might as well know it now. Your real friends will come to respect and love you for your honesty and truthfulness.

No need now to plan your conversation ahead of time, such as, "If he says this to me, I will say that to him." Keep the faith; whatever it is, overlook it. Be plain-spoken with firmness, kindness and patience. Wait for the moment and discover what to say and do—if anything.

Make sure you overlook the things that should be overlooked and are plain-spoken about those things that should be said. Don't close your eyes to evil. See it and don't resent it.

Be sure you do not change your words to soften the outcome, keeping things to yourself that should be said or done before they fester into resentment or guilt.

Whatever personal problem you have, there is no need to analyze it any longer. You will see the solution in its own time. By digging around in your past and peering into the future, you confuse yourself more. Keep meditating so as to become objective, and then as you come to the light you will perceive the cause of all your troubles.

You should not analyze these words and their author's intent. Instead, think about it until you understand it deeply. Just keep relating to and remembering the basic premise, which is to be patient with injustice and be plainspoken where it is wise to speak up.

It does not matter if people love you. You love them. It

does not matter if people understand you. You understand them. And if they do not forgive you, you forgive them.

Do not say, "Stupid idiot!" when you see someone who is acting foolish. Let your attitude say, "Here, let me help you." Observe their faults, but do not emotionally puff up or resent them for this. Make allowances right on the spot.

Do not take personal offense at anything. Let criticism roll off you like water off a duck's back. Be not excited by praise or offended by criticism, and don't be too eager to give praise or criticism.

Now, to sum up: you must meditate because you want to, not because you have to. Remember to overlook on the spot and be outspoken with firmness, kindness and patience from now on, keeping this principle uppermost in your thoughts in the ever-present. Do not worry or dwell on the past or the future. Let past memories rise to the surface and face what you must in the light without resenting what you see or struggling to change it.

Do your exercise, and the exercise will provide the energy to keep understanding alive in you—which basically is to be patient and to be plain-spoken.

Each time you are patient and do not respond to torment and temptation, there will be a sense of achievement; you will see things in a different light, and what you will come to understand will increase the meaning of the basic truth, which is to overlook on the spot. Then, each time you do your exercise, you will automatically carry down your new understanding

17

into your daily life so that you will do it with increasing skill the next time, which in turn will bring more understanding to you. Thus, the more you understand, the more you feel inclined to do what you understand, and the less you will respond to outer conditions, temptation and what people say or do.

Nothing must be added to this concept while you do this exercise, nor anything taken away from it. Merely be reminded to overlook on the spot and be outspoken with firmness, kindness and patience.

It is not intended that you should not think of anything else. As you go through your daily chores and come into contact with people, no matter what you do, no matter what you feel and think, do everything in accord with the principles of overlooking on the spot and being outspoken with firmness, kindness and patience.

HAVE COMPASSION

You should make allowances for people with all your thinking, all your feeling, with all your understanding, because you want to, not because you have to.

Remember, do not analyze. Ponder on it, within yourself. Do not worry. Cast out doubt. Bring your mind back again and again to the objective state of being in the now present and observe doubt flee from you. Don't discuss this with anyone yet. There are no words. Just think it and feel it secretly and do it.

Now begin slowly to pull back from this reading. You may feel a little tired. Give yourself a good long stretch.

Remember to do your exercise at least three times a day as you have been instructed. The exercise is very important, along with the basic concept of patience.

NOTE: The author cautions the reader to interpret the word "overlook" in the dictionary sense he intended, namely, "to pass over without censure or judgment; to excuse." The word "overlook" can be, and often is, used to mean "to ignore; to disregard completely," but to ignore anything at all as though it did not exist would run counter to one of the primary objectives of meditation, which is to develop a heightened awareness of reality, to see everything as it is, but without being tempted to judge it emotionally. Therefore, the reminder to "overlook" is simply a reminder to discern without judgment.

*Also, notice the special way the author wishes you to concentrate. In your past experience, concentration always involved effort of will, and that involved you with the thoughts to which you are now fixated. All of the interests you have concentrated upon are now fascinations and fixations. You are a slave to them without even realizing it, because through your fixated attention you even forgot how to realize. Thus if the author asked you to concentrate, you would end up doing more of what you have always done wrong. Instead, he wants you merely to **notice** yourself and your thoughts.*

2

Understanding the Process of Meditation
and What We Might Expect from Meditation

The meditation, properly used, will bring about a significant change in your relationship with words. Whereas you have been accustomed to respond to words as though they themselves were the idea or the thing referred to, you will soon find yourself responding increasingly to the meaning that the word reawakens in you. You will come to realize that at various times in your life you have been "hung up" on words, studies, concepts and ideologies. You have allowed words to drive you and to shape your behavior.

Oh, how we have labored in the past for our pride food: a few kind words. How defenseless we have been when unkind words, words of condemnation, have threatened our "word castles" and made it impossible for us to disagree without becoming disagreeable. And how confusing it all is! Concepts we have learned and accepted as true are threatened constantly by opposing worldly theories and opinions. We have even rebelled against "good" words that painfully puffed up our ego and made too many agonizing demands on us in the living up to them, and wound up leading us further away from any real good rather than toward it. We have shied away from these "good" words and embraced the bad ones, for they at least are more honest in their association of the bad label (word) with the bad deed (reality).

Once the word begins to motivate, it begins also to substitute for real meaning and purpose. The process that it sets in motion is called brainwashing. Its victim develops an appetite for words, using them as filling, a source of comfort and direction, a camouflage for spiritual emptiness and confusion.

Another unwholesome relationship we have with words is the "allergic" one. We become so sensitive to them—as we notice the pain they can cause and our helplessness against them—that we can hardly bear to have anything to do with them at all. Study becomes difficult, if not impossible, and all verbal communication seems to threaten us.

Perhaps you labor to make people eat their words, hoping thereby to destroy the effect of their words upon you. But you are laboring *for* the word or *against* the word, and you are not living truly. You are still not moving or having your being from the reality that words such as these were designed to lead you to. You have allowed people to lead you *with* truth instead of *to* Truth.

As a result of the meditation exercise, your consciousness will begin to reject words as meaning or as motivating forces. You may experience an emptying of thought content in this respect. You may experience forgetfulness both of trivia (grudges, for instance) and of important matters (for which you have no immediate and pressing need). Chatter, names, babble, excuses, false concepts and commercials vanish.

True concepts that you once accepted without understanding will come back for review and be energized by conscious acceptance. To the degree that we accept, we energize, so that words derive their power from the fact that they are driven by, and associated with, meaning and insight.

Before the time of understanding, we were all brainwashed. We played back noises like parrots; we mumbled acceptable phrases in order not to rock the boat. We never spoke from meaning. We never spoke honestly. We didn't want to displease others, for to do so would cut off our supply of words of praise. So we gave our associates the words that they also wanted to hear.

We needed words and the sources of the words. We became increasingly dependent upon and identified with our word sources, until, very often, our needfulness stirred our pride to rebellion against them. Then, our resentment made us guilty, our guilt made us afraid, and soon we were lost and wrong, unable to find our way back to simple beingness.

You will not have been meditating long before old long-cherished beliefs will start coming back to you for re-examination by the light of new understanding. In some of them you will see deeper meaning than you could have dreamed possible before. The words will be the same as they were, but they will unlock the door to a brand new world of awareness. In others, you will see the fatal flaw, the appeal to pride and ambition, and you will be able to reject them without effort. Actually, they will disperse as any other shadow would when you turn the light of truth on them. Suddenly, words will be tools for your use, no longer ends in themselves— and it will be a great relief. To the degree that you are able consciously to accept or reject words and concepts from the framework of real meaning, to that degree will you inherit control over language, and language will cease to control you. But to the degree that you allow impressions to enter your mind unconsciously, to that degree are you controlled by words, knowledge and the cunning powers-that-be which feed you the line as they rob you of life.

There are invisible "sticky" fibers of communication that link reaction, feeling and thought together. Your conscious awareness is also chained to due process of thought. When you meditate, you will become conscious of a sudden shift in viewpoint as these thought processes tend to pull you down into them via these invisible connections. As you pull back out and away from the involvement with dream and thought stuff, that threadlike connection is broken. Our consciousness is made aware of the effect of the thought stuff tugging at it by means of a mystical relationship with Reality, which, in effect, pulls it back to view those thoughts and their power to drag our attention down.

Our compulsions to err are made up of many such patterns. As you become aware of them and successfully wrestle with them to break their hold, older patterns will emerge in the form of distractions and bona fide guilts. These may tend to pull you down from your position of observing them, and excite you to deal angrily with them. But remember: never be angry over what you see. Anger only strengthens the tie, involves you more closely with the process, and separates you from reason. *You will find that you can dissolve distractions and trivia that try to get in the way of your concentration, but be careful not to try to resolve the real faults that rise to your view. Just allow them to bother you, look at them, be aware of them, but don't try to deal with them in any way.*

What appear to be suggestions in the meditation exercise actually are *not intended* to be. The words do not exhort you

LIKE MY AWARENESS OF EVIL POSSESSION THAT COMPELS ME TO EAT COMPULSIVELY WHAT I DON'T EVEN WANT & DON'T EVEN ENJOY — LIKE COCONUT MILK FROZEN DESSERT 2/21/12

24

to be patient; rather, they *remind* you of your need of patience. If the meditation became hypnotic, you would find yourself merely acting out the role of the patient person, just as many persons act out a religious role when inspired by their church. But there is a great deal of difference between religious excitement and religious experience. Religious excitement is hypnotic and precludes the real experience.

Most of us are mesmerized already, moving excitedly, believing in our piety. But this appears as hypocrisy in the eyes of others. It creates more emotional disturbances to be soothed and mesmerized away by still more religious excitement. People who live this way feel guilty about not going to church or other elected establishments. If the cassettes, or the reading of the meditation exercise, were hypnotic, it would have a similar effect on you. However, with the right intent, the meditation concentration relates you back to reason and neutralizes the hypnotic state that you are presently in, so that it becomes possible to reason with you without impressing you with words about reason.

You might become angry at the meditation because you have misused it, hoping that it would supply you with your need, whereas it has only revealed your need, error and helplessness. Acknowledgement of need is part of the spiritual process of meditation, perfecting the humiliation of the soul by degrees; through that need are we fulfilled mystically.

The needs of a proud mind are different from those of the humble mind. A proud mind needs the hypnosis of temptation and excitement, both for the accomplishment of egocentric goals and for the disguising of the guilt that results from such goal-seeking masked by false piety (religious excitement). A sinister force attends those needs and enslaves us to them. But the repentant mind signals a need for correction that is

25

attended by God. What qualifies us is our awareness of our lack (failing), and that arises initially from hungering and thirsting after truth. In the light of the attending truth, we can see and be sorry about our cruel pride and its vain emotional needs (for kicks), and then we can be changed.

The concentration exercise helps you to discover this truth; first, by helping you to relate back to reality. To clarify: a consciousness that is sincerely seeking is a consciousness qualified for life. The meditation enables that life to flow into your mind and body and effect an inner rapport or wholeness. With your emotional equipment "idling," so to speak, you are not so reactive to ideas. You do not suffer the pain of moving excited by those ideas that would fall into the "religious excitement" category. The suggestions presented only reawaken you to your Self (conscience), which has already been declaring to you much the same thing. Now, instead of being moved by words, you will be moved by the realization and power that reply to your true need.

If thoughts do not cloud your mind, you can see a light shining in your consciousness. This light is not the same as sunlight, but it does serve a similar function in that it makes our character flower as the solar rays make the plants grow. When you were small, you may have seen those moving energy patterns of color in your mind and wondered what they were. But as you grew, the excitement of the world rose up in your mind as thoughts and pictures, and soon the light faded.

But the light is still shining in your darkness. It appears as conscience when you err. Before the time of error, what you now know as conscience was a clear, untroubled consciousness, containing the pattern of your potential. You often felt it as a pressure behind your mind trying to tell you something. It

26

was the light that should have shaped your behavior. When you became impatient with its promptings and looked to the outside world for guidance, it became troubled by your faithlessness. It is that troubled state of consciousness that we all know as "conscience."

Conscience is the light that shines on our rabid thoughts and allows us to see our mistakes; but if we are proud, we do not want to see them, so we bend all our efforts toward putting out the light within us that would show us our faults. We have physical eyes to see where we are physically going, but the light that shines in our consciousness tells us what is right and wrong and illuminates our spiritual path.

If we do not want correction or right direction, the light of consciousness (or the afterglow of conscience) is an abomination to us, and we must try to put it out. But it isn't easy to put out that light. The means we most frequently employ are anger, excitement and mental imaging.

In nature, plants have a built-in mechanism for converting sunlight into growth energy. Each plant converts the light to its own use according to its own seed pattern; that is, grass seed will produce grass and dandelion seeds will produce dandelions. Now, the light not only provides the energy for growth; it also gives the signal for growth. In other words, it actually "turns the plant on."

Just as the sunlight provides turn-on value for plants, danger provides turn-on value for animals. This "danger" is usually signaled by the presence of another animal, the other animal being a modified light form. The sphere of influence (auric radiation) surrounding the intruder affects the animal in much the same way as sunlight affects the plant, in that it provides the impetus for growth. In this way, we see that animals grow and take shape as a result of their inter-

27

relationships, the losers providing fuel (food) for the victors. They derive their energy and turn-on value from one another in precisely the same way as the plant derives energy and turn-on value from sunlight; but because they are more complex organisms, the principle operates in a more complicated and evolved way.

Now what about man? Nobody in whom the light of consciousness still shines can honestly believe that man is simply the most highly-evolved of the animals, designed to take his turn-on value from other people, for then we could never be any better than those who turn us on. We know intuitively that, as people, we must live in the world, but not be of it. We must obtain its support and nourishment without allowing it to dictate our pattern of growth. In other words, we must take and retain dominion over the things of the earth. As people, the closest link we have with reality is our consciousness. Through this consciousness, the Light who sired all creation outside touches us inside and turns us off to outside influences that seek to control us.

While we were turned on to the world, we were both controlled and shaped by the world's dark light. We not only were not masters of our environment; we were slaves to the impulses that rose in us as replies to pressures and passions. Now, if we are willing to see by the light that shines through the lens of consciousness, we can see the harsh outlines of our dark thoughts and wrong responses to the world. We will see how our desire to live egocentrically forced us to resort to light-dimming methods and associations.

We have chosen our friends and associates cleverly and carefully (though perhaps subconsciously) on the basis of their ability and willingness to help us put out the light. They have told us, by words or implication, how great we are; they have

28

pretended not to see our faults (they can); and their dishonesty has excited us. We have needed other people to reflect back to us a good image of ourselves, and we have paid them in advance by giving them a good opinion of themselves.

The "heat waves" bouncing back and forth between us and other lovers of darkness flatter us and excite our imagination. For a short time, at least, they "out-shout" the light of consciousness. But when money is spent and excitement subsides and it is the "morning after the night before," that other light appears again in the form of pressure, uneasiness, conflict or conscience.

One of the things that light is trying to show us is that men should not be trying to live with and from each other in the manner of animals, for that way leads to war, fear, disease and death. Rather, our relationships with one another should agree with the light that we all share. The character-modifying effect of the light in each of us makes us gracious, just and able to cooperate with one another toward an ultimate good, without becoming enslaved to one another's demands and need to look good. We should not be serving the beast in one another; we should be serving the Light who made us all.

The conscious mind, being our closest link with God, is fashioned to "see" and move by the light of reality. Such motion, originating through and flowing out of the self, is harmonious with purpose, a soothing balm to the restless nature. It is incompatible with egotism. But when we allow pressures of the world to upset us away from the quiet consciousness through emotional reaction, then our inherited factor of pride rushes to the defense of our compulsive behavior, justifies it and gives us the illusion that we are living our own life.

The process of programming by pressure seems natural

enough, since it duplicates closely the purpose for which the mind was created, except for one big difference; we feel guilty about it. And we feel guilty because man, unlike the lower animals, is inner-related by nature.

All outside-related creatures are in harmony with outside stimulus and grow in accordance with the order that controls them. Growth is always fleshly, and animal vitality is renewed by daily contact with external pressures. This kind of "renewing" for man causes him to grow in a beastly way and develops thoughts and cravings in him that he knows (by the light he is trying to put out) to be inferior, unseemly for one of his nature. But being egocentric, he cannot admit to inferiority or error, so he sets about to erase the evidence of his error. As he strives to justify himself, he must also justify the process that caused him to err, so until the time of salvation, we are blind to the power that controls us. Excited by outer pressure, the conscience is blinded.

The conscious mind of man must be still before the subconscious can be impressed by it, and the consciousness of man cannot be still until it becomes aware of its restless ambitious nature and turns from its worldly pursuits. Once it is committed, no longer reaching out after things and activities to obscure the presence of truth, it will become still and in the stillness it will see the light.

When we are able to see by the true light, we see not only our own hidden thoughts, but the intents of those we have justified and "loved" (needed). Until that time, we remain blind for two reasons: our ego refuses to see, and our emotions are attached to error. We cannot see the forces that control us because we are egocentric and simply refuse to see that we are wrong. As we justify our faults, we also justify that which made the fault grow in us, so what is really all wrong seems to us to be all right. As we grow more excited, we fall further. Again we shield ourselves from the correction of the conscience. Our mind grows dark. We cannot see because excuses and excitements, imagery and distractions shut out the light that would otherwise have illuminated our path and put an end to our groping and guessing through life.

Bear in mind that the hand-raising feature of the meditation exercise is only a means to an end. The process of imagery is designed to inaugurate a chain reaction of responses touched off by conscious awareness. When your hand begins to rise, it is evidence of an energy value originating within you. But once you discover that by concentration through the middle of your forehead you can effect bodily responses, then imagery is no longer necessary. Once the principle has proven itself to you, thinking of your arm rising might actually inhibit the appearance of new understanding. Remember too that bringing the attention to the middle of the forehead does not imply any physical movement of the eyes. Looking upward will cause eyestrain and headaches. This important technicality may mark the fine line of difference between success and frustration.

Just being aware of the patterns of light and color that you see in your mind, and projecting them into the tingling of your hands, is all that is necessary. When silly images and thoughts start dancing in your mind to distract you from the process of observing them, simply superimpose the light pattern over them.

The patterns of light are etheric "computer" data that replace the lying imagination and its excuse-making proclivities. They affect every cell and nerve fiber in your being. They are the reverse of the light waves of environmental pressure that affect your body adversely. As they reverse the negative effects of (pressure,) they impart an intelligent pattern of unfoldment. They cancel out the wild, unreasonable responses to unreasonable external pressures.

The evidence of a Higher Presence in meditation is a change in breathing. If you were under outside pressure, and responding to it, your breathing would manifest this also.

With concentration, you inherit power to break the pattern of thought stuff that holds you to unwanted habit patterns. Usually, thought patterns are excuses and justifications for past errors. They form a hard protective shell around the faults, but you can break that shell by being aware of the light as opposed to being caught up in thought. (This light is the truth,) which will provide a shield that error cannot pierce.

We have no power over what comes up from the depths as the shell is broken. It may be like opening a can of worms unexpectedly. Suffer the pain of remorse. (Resist the temptation) to hide from or to change what you see. (The pain) of such an experience will give rise to (a true desire) to be different, and that helplessness and wishing is the call to salvation.

In time, (a new energy) comes in reply. It is the light that shineth upon every man who comes into the world. It is the light that still shines in the darkness, and the darkness comprehendeth it not.

I FELT THAT NIGHT 3/21 AFTER I WAS AWAY OF THE EVIL FORCE BEHIND MY BINGE

THE OBJECT OF MEDITATION

The primary objective of the concentration is to cause the emotions and the intellect to respond to the quiet consciousness. Then when difficult situations present themselves, our unclouded, impartial understanding will see what is right.

Our biggest problem is an active consciousness. The active

consciousness is like a windswept sea. We are unable to gaze beyond its disturbed surface into what is true. This, basically, is a problem of the ego, in that our consciousness desires to become its own arranger of purpose and order. This type of mind is rebellious toward the purpose prepared for it to rediscover. It is always planning and seeking its own goals. A consciousness that is active is blind to what is true, and is therefore forced to make unwise decisions, with only limited outer knowledge to rely upon.

Knowledge then becomes the source material for decision. But decisions arrived at by this means can never be correct, because all unseeing decisions sever us further from our true purpose. A mind forced to make decisions is always in conflict with itself, and from frustration and anger, a mist arises in the mind that further clouds our reason. First we have conflict, but as we make excuses and establish those excuses as "truth," we have confusion.

In contrast, the mind that sees the futility of choosing its own pathway through life, through waiting patiently and watching, will become tranquil, able to perceive what is true. This is patience, or "waiting without agony."

In perceiving what is right for each moment, by the light, we begin to see a new pattern of action come into being. Is there any choosing in the matter of the course that your body will follow when you see where you are going? It is only ambition that leads us to deny our spiritual commitment to, and unfoldment from, the light of truth.

In meditation we concentrate upon our hands. Then we extend the light to affect our thoughts. This slows down the pace of intellect and calms our restless emotions. We are then able to desensitize our body to unreasonable pressures. We slow down the spinning compulsive analysis that once led that proud, blind, decision-making ego further away from reality. We fast from the excitement that we once craved to set our bodies into motion toward our dreams (ambitions). Gradually, as we give up the stimulation that supports our pride, we shall receive a new direction and impetus for living.

When you thus enter into life, and trials and tribulations come your way—then, because of that quietness and inner control, you will cease to react as before. You will merely observe. In observing, you will see the exact meaning of the moment, receiving insight for the correct moves, in words or in deeds. Now, because of the discipline that you have practiced in the exercise by the expansion of consciousness, what you realize for that moment will become your directive. The realization becomes energized into feeling, and then into action. If the consciousness learns patiently to observe life, then every action, word and thought shall always be correct. And consciousness will never become conscience again.

It will not be possible for our minds to become still until that consciousness realizes that its role is one of an inactive, obedient observer. Then the intellect will become corrected to a new role, trained to move by the light that shows us the way. The hunger for excessive amounts of intellectual knowledge is symbolic of an unseeing, rebellious mind without light, compensating with knowledge, a mind playing God. Such a mind will know only unbearable conflict, fear and guilt.

The concentration allows for an inward pressure. Such stimulation, not of this world, will add a new quality to your nature. Perhaps the only thing you will notice is the tingling of the fingers, a change in breathing, movements of the face, skull and skin. Just as daily upsets produce a growing variety of problems, so will the daily dose of inward stimulation provide a growing "complex" of changes for the better, as earthly stimulations are replaced by the motivation from within. You may notice the old dying nature reappearing in thought. As your breathing was affected by outer pressure, so it is now affected by inner pressure.

The second stage of meditation can become a thought-observing process.

The third stage of meditation can become pain to the consciousness inasmuch as we shall be bothered by what we have allowed to transpire in us in the past. Do not deal with these thoughts or feelings. Do not attempt to change them. Just watch the pain that comes from the observation of them. This is called repentance. You must allow its pain and acknowledge your lack, for any attempt to deal with your old thoughts and feelings merely sickens you and duplicates the egocentric "coping" that confused you in the first place. Tears may come at this stage—the body may tremble in what seems to be fear. Still do nothing. If your pride is not willing to be humbled in this fashion, and is unwilling to receive the essence of new life—if it desires to continue its own cause—you will find yourself in trouble for meditating for the wrong motive.

You may find that you will relive certain past experiences mentally, emotionally and physically. When you begin to recognize the cause of past problems, be sure you do not resent seeing them come to light. Merely observe what is revealed, and be glad to see the suppressed layers come to the surface again to be reviewed. Disturbing as they may be, do not resent or deal with them. It is this pain that leads to repentance.

Having acknowledged your errors, and having taken back the blame that you had cast upon others, you will eventually feel relief from your burden. As you go through these experiences, of course, you will feel a great travail; but afterwards come joy, a sense of going forward and a renewed sense of purpose.

All of us have hidden from our weakness, which we covered up by a series of excuses, distractions and suppressions. We have built layers of distracting wrong thoughts, emotions and activities in an attempt to conceal, mask or compensate for our inner weaknesses and failings. We have built up those useless and vain ways of life through past habit patterns that are designed to mask our inferiority, our fears and our guilts. Our activities have thus been built upon false values; our habits are mechanical movements to ease the pain of living out of step.

You may see what you have done wrong in the past. As your life unfolds before you, do not resent seeing these things; do not cover them up again, as you did before, but willingly suffer the agony of your soul. The repentance that results from this pain is a godly sorrow—"Blessed are they that mourn, for they shall be comforted."

To be honestly sorry for what you have done requires that you recognize what it is that was wrong. When this happens, you will learn your lesson and be relieved of the burden and the need to make up for past mistakes. The nature of true love does not require you to be lashed into the impossible agony of "making up" for all your past mistakes. Many of those whom you have done wrong are dead. Many others would not accept your apology, or they would only use your willingness to make up to them for their own selfish gain. If you truly loved people, you would not require them to make up for their every mistake, would you? You would simply be glad they had recognized their wrong and repented of it. You would be content to see them live life as it should be lived, from that moment onward. So when you discover what is wrong, refuse to hide from it, justify it or blame someone or something for it—then you are truly sorry and repentant. In this is found the relief of burden. Each self-admission of error brings you closer to release from it. From now on, acknowledge wrong motive (wrong intent) each moment.

The meditation exercise will teach you to respond to your own conscience. It will enable that consciousness of what is realized for each moment to function. Henceforth, there will be no more guilt to be excused and covered. Simply acknowledging a wrong motive can change that motive, even though the action may remain the same. If you can continue any path of action without guilt, without emotional support, after having observed a wrong motive, it is a sure indication that the motive has been made right.

If you have procured a copy of the cassettes and are using them as a guide to your meditation—or if you are using this book, alone or with the help of a friend—you will notice that the words in the discussion portion of the exercise merely bear witness to the truth that you always knew in your own heart. However, you never responded to that truth. Now that you are allowing yourself to be reminded of it, you will find yourself thinking, "Why didn't I listen to myself? Why did I listen to other people?" (You were excited and tempted by them because they supported your pride and ambitions.) The words you hear (or read) will bear witness to the reality within you, and the meditation will enable you to bridge the gap to your understanding, so that you will be enabled to walk in response to inward urging, living and loving the way you should have done, placing justice and fairness before all.

Do not be afraid. The same power that reveals truth to a willingly obedient consciousness and body will also give you the power to express it and to bear the certain tribulations that must inevitably follow. Previously you lived to escape the condemnation of people—earning an inward condemnation instead. In getting along with people, you could not get along with yourself.

Perhaps your old sickness will return to you. Do not be alarmed; it only appears to return. In reality, you were never cured in the first place. Whatever methods you employed in the past to "cure" yourself only covered the symptoms, or suppressed the expression of the disease. Perhaps you had an ulcer, and you had your stomach removed. That did not cure the disease, for the cause is still there, finding new areas of expression. Without the understanding of cause, you go to the grave on the installment plan, a piece at a time: a gland, a lung, a gall bladder, and so on. Do not willfully stop your medications, however. Meditate, and in time you will find your medication giving you up, without any expenditure of effort on your part. Be patient, and allow your faith to grow.

Correct meditation is the only non-habit "habit" that you will have. At any time, you may choose to stop meditation and return to your old ways. Each day your subjection to God is a free-will offering of mind and body; in it you exchange weakness for strength and doubt for faith.

The "spirit" of alcohol compels the alcoholic. He is not free to choose to refrain, because he is addicted to the call of feeling and emotion. Be warned, therefore; improper meditation techniques will cause a similar addiction, through the oblivion that they offer. If you meditate only for relief of your agony, then you must necessarily, though subconsciously, create a problem or a pain for the pleasurable contrast that relief will bring. You will be meditating for the wrong reason—for symptomatic relief from being tense, sick and afraid. Herein lies the danger of becoming a "meditationcoholic"; angry and upset at the diminishing results, you will become fixated to meditation through the need for the relief or escape it might bring.

Correct meditation prevents the tension that arises from emotional reaction. If you are becoming upset, then meditating for relief of that upset, you will not be meditating as you should. When you are meditating for the right reason (to *be* better, not to *feel* better), you meet life without the building up of tension—it just is not there to need relieving. You will then be relieved of the need to drink and smoke; yes, even the need to meditate! You can then meditate without abnormal need for relief. Your meditation will then become an offering. Note the difference: when the "need" for relief falls away, we are free to meditate simply because it is wise, and prodding is no longer necessary.

Be careful that you do not claim each improvement as a personal accomplishment. This tends to build up your ego, causing it to exalt itself and become proud. Do not become excited when you see your habits giving you up; also, take care not to look down upon those who are still struggling with their vices. Any exaltation of the ego, and stimulation to our ego, separates us from the truth and causes tension. Your only objective should be true humility, a growing willingness to respond to what is right and not to *be* that right.

You will discover an unaccustomed spontaneity in what you say and do in each moment. You will cease analyzing and judging the rightness, wrongness or effects of your words and actions. Now when you look back, you will see that what you said and did in a natural, spontaneous way was motivated by the outside world rather than your own intuition; therefore, it was always wrong—and kept you busy trying to justify it!

Now you will marvel at the natural flow of human grace

at all times. You will see the correctness in all your actions, far beyond your own capacity to plan for in advance of each moment. In your new correctness, you will see that you are having a different effect upon other people, and you will observe the intellectual reason for the new state of affairs. This is how you will learn—by obeying, observing, marveling and believing.

SERVING THE PRESENCE
IN THE PRESENT

To the extent that you meet the present with the "Presence" of mind, love and patience—to that extent will your past repressed errors bubble to the surface for review and be corrected in the present. You see, the present is the place where we become strong or weak. If we find enough understanding to recognize that our past mistakes have been carried over to the present; if we endeavor to notice them and allow them to be conquered in that present—we shall then have the strength and sinew of mind, body and emotion with which to allow those repressed memories to come out of hiding.

The same virtue that strengthens you, and conquers your weakness in each present moment, will call out of hiding those ancient hatreds and fears that you once lacked the strength to conquer, and therefore repressed.

When we reacted to life without virtue, we saw our ugly animal nature rising to the consciousness. Unable to overcome the growing legion of horrors evoked in each experience, we repressed our knowledge of them, hoping in this way to free ourselves from conflict. Perhaps we excused these wrong actions, perhaps we compensated for them; but whatever mechanics we employed, we still hid from seeing what we could not change or conquer.

Your meditation will cause you to see your old problems rising to the surface in a very special, bearable order. At first you may be disturbed or concerned, but you should not be angry. Next, you will be grateful, for what now sees these things is far different from what once saw them. When we no longer beat against our problems as they return, and when the seeing of them is a joy rather than an agony, then we are free! One day there will be no more past to see—just a very happy and blessed present.

WHAT WE MIGHT EXPECT FROM MEDITATION

1. The meditation causes chemical changes within the body as poisons are expelled. You may experience a cold that lingers as poisonous substances are ejected. You may notice a change in bowel habits and other bodily functions.

2. In the beginning you may experience an outburst of emotion as suppressed feelings rise to the surface to be recognized—and dissolved in the light of consciousness.

3. Cold shivers, occasional perspiration and labored or heavy breathing reveal contact-response to a higher consciousness. It means that something has been added that is causing changes to occur.

4. You will receive a mild feeling of stimulation, almost

like that provided by a shot of brandy. Upon opening your eyes after meditation, you will experience a clean feeling within; even the outside world appears more clear and bright.

5. You will perceive a fading away of past memories as they come to be replaced with more valuable realizations of the present, which then blossom into a steady flow of new thoughts.

6. Time ceases to be important. As the need to rush disappears, you become more efficient in the use of your energy. Time becomes eternally abundant and renewed, whereas previously you never had enough time, and felt that it was running out.

7. You will accomplish many times the amount of work in any given period than was your custom; yet you will have the strange feeling that you have not done any work at all. You will be attended by a joyful sense of eternal living.

8. At times you may feel as though you were wearing a tight skullcap on your head. You may feel your face tightening up as the lax muscles contract, revealing the presence of inner discipline and love.

9. Occasionally you will feel suspended in space, as if your body had melted into the universe and become one with all nature.

10. Flashes of insight will occur frequently from now on. You will find yourself expressing wisdom and knowl-

edge that you never outwardly learned or heard before. Your own mouth will become the teacher to your ears, and your physical self will gasp with wonderment.

11. You will experience an eager desire to tell all this to a world that is not yet ready. Careful. You may fall into anger again when people fail to understand your beautiful world, a dimension they are unable to see. Be sure that you do not mouth your new understanding prematurely, before it has had time to become part of you in experience, for you will feel guilty if you do. Only when you have suffered practice in what you now realize can you dare to explain it to others. Without practice, you possess no authority with which to teach or to show. Even if you speak truth, the effect will be the reverse of what you intended.

12. Some people become frightened by the meditation technique, for it represents a choice between two ways of life. It reveals what we should be, and cuts the excuses, once and for all.

13. Many people will hate the whole idea of meditation. They will hate you as well for seeing through their nice illusion of goodness. Now, having heard the word, or having seen the truth in action through you, they can no longer excuse their failure to find God and reality, for it was before them and they denied it. Their hatred becomes a hatred of truth, and they must forever struggle to destroy the light that burns in His presence. To hate that light in you is to hate it in themselves. It will cause a conflict that can never be put out.

14. You will discover friends as enemies, and enemies as real friends. Your whole life will change as the vultures fall away and you draw new and finer acquaintances into your orbit.

15. You will continue to grow quietly in stature and in grace, in virtue and perhaps even in worldly possessions, without expending any effort toward that end. Your enemies will also grow, in their confusion and fear. Therefore, have compassion on your enemies, for they will nourish and strengthen you, and you may help them eventually.

16. The good things will be good, and the bad things will provide benefit; not only momentarily, but in the form of courage to face bigger trials, which lead to the "pot of gold" on the other side of matter. Men without virtue are frightened by the unknown. Therefore, they cannot "come over" or overcome any experience properly. They remain forever subject to the world through their emotional reactions (primarily fear, triggered by guilt).

17. You may experience strange sensations in different parts of your body as healing takes place. Different stages of development create different individual experiences, too numerous to catalog here.

18. The leveling-off period, or periods, may last from weeks to years before new layers of awareness unfold. Each new stratum of consciousness is entered only when we have successfully traveled through the strata preceding it.

19. Sometimes you will hear, quite distinctly, words "spo-

ken" to you in short phrases. Do not be alarmed. These phrases may startle you, and they may seem to have no immediate value. You will remember them vividly, however, and wonder about them, until some later experience shows you their meaning. The phrases with immediate, obvious value contain hidden motives and suppressed memories that are rising to the surface to be dissolved through recognition.

When we seek truth and understanding, we suddenly begin to see life as it really is. We see ourselves for what we really are; we see what is required of us and what we are required to give up. We may not wish to continue on the path of truth for this reason. At this point, we may actually see our hatred of truth. But if you also see that there is no other way but to do what your conscience requires, then you are safe—the choice has been made. If you choose not to continue in the right way, then you must fight your conscience,with the full realization that you hate reality. Your latter state will be worse than the former!

The exercise should never be learned by heart like a poem. While the monologue is explaining the idea during the meditation, keep your mind concentrated on your hand regardless of whether you remember the presentation or not. In this fashion you will discover that you will casually understand what you are told; but you will not be able to learn mechanically. This way, the information reawakens an inner knowing so that you will gain more and more understanding each time you listen. During the course of the day you will receive flashes of insight. Refrain from trying to recall these later, for each flash of insight replaces the erroneous and unconscious patterns of thinking you held previously. This, cumulatively, changes your outlook and reactions, preparing you for further awareness and understanding.

Do not worry if your hand fails to rise during the exercise, for the hand-raising is only a preliminary indication to measure the success of the concentration. Just a mild, tingling, prickly sensation in your hand is all that is needed.

You may discover that the exercise appears to lose its effectiveness, or becomes more difficult, as you progress. This is an illusion. It arises simply because you have shifted to another state of being without fully realizing it; becoming acclimated to this state, you will lose the pleasurable sharp relief from your former pains.

There is a tremendous contrast of relief after the first exercise or so, but after the novelty wears off, you might be looking for improved feelings to prove to yourself that you are doing the exercise properly. If it does not feel the same as it did the first time, you may lose heart. This is a common error, and it is often made a day or two after the first exercise. You may also start to worry, and if this happens you might revert back to your old way of thinking. For the moment, remember that peace of mind is not an emotional feeling. You will understand this as you grow in awareness.

Very soon after you have started to meditate, you may be startled to discover that people (especially members of your family) are acting differently toward you. At times, it will seem that you can almost see through them as far as their motives are concerned. This is because your attitude has changed and you are no longer reacting to people; they are reacting to you.

The exercise leaves you with a strong sense of awareness to which you will become accustomed. The greater the light of your understanding and awareness, the greater your self-control.

The meditation exercise produces a response to the inner self. It is a counter-hypnosis to the hypnosis of the world. Hypnosis is produced as a result of an emotional response to external pressure, which makes you receptive to suggestion. It capitalizes on some existing gullibility or desire. The more you are upset, the more you are hypnotized and the less you are in command of yourself.

The meditation exercise leads you back to your inner self. If you teach someone to walk, you certainly do not expect to have to walk for him. He must be able to walk alone. So it is with the exercise. It is a do-it-yourself project that creates control from within and in so doing cancels our compulsive responses to the outside world.

Be sure to do the exercise the first thing each morning, before any other thing, to prepare you for the day. Do not make the mistake of waiting too long, having a reaction to some experience, and then doing the exercise—in which case you will have it back to front. You will be trying to ease symptoms (results) rather than preventing the cause.

The meditation exercise will never become a habit. By choosing to do this exercise each morning you choose rightly for that day. This choice frees you from compulsive patterned ideas and actions. Failure to do the exercise constitutes choosing the old ways again.

The exercise will embrace and extend the positive conscious knowledge already within—but if you do this exercise with the idea of getting something out of it, it will magnify your selfishness and lead to disappointment. Everything you "learn" as a result of the meditation exercise is what you already know; the only thing new about it is the way it enters the mind and feelings from within—because you wish it to be thus, rather than having been pressured to accept it.

If you do this exercise for the purpose of overcoming a problem through your own will, you are trying to remove symptoms and ignoring the cause. If you persist in this egocentric willfulness and yet succeed in the meditation exercise, it will be because you are hypnotizing yourself with the exercise and not actually meditating at all. Sooner or later you will become aware of this self-deception, and a terrible fear will be added to the problems you already have. So watch your motivation—keep it pure.

At this point, the author has already given you the key to your inner self, prepared you for possible side effects, and warned you of the dangers inherent in its wrong use. The remaining chapters of the book are to be regarded more as a sharing of insight than a teaching. If you are meditating, much of it will be heard as an echo of your own observation. The words that follow are the fruits of the author's own meditation, recorded here for whatever use you care to make of them. It is his feeling that you will find excerpts from some of the chapters helpful as material for conscious listening or reading preparatory to doing the meditation exercise. (Some of the material is available on audio cassettes, which may be obtained at the Foundation of Human Understanding.) Or you may wish to have certain passages read to you as background material during the exercise. But by all means, remember to do the exercise frequently by yourself in the course of the day. If you begin to think you need the inspirational material to get in the mood to meditate, lay it aside for awhile and give some careful thought to your motivation—you may be looking for external balm rather than inner direction. Remember that it is your own meditation that will reestablish your connection with your true self and provide you with your own insight. Seek the Kingdom of Heaven within yourself, for that is where you will find it.

By the way, you may find the following material extremely negative. The author is more interested in exposing the evil, dissecting the sacred cows and cutting away the brambles that have separated you from reality, than in telling you what that reality is. But if you will think about it a moment, you will realize that he has no alternative. What would you think of him if, after telling you that you must find reality within yourself, he proceeded to rob you of the discovery by telling you all about it?

3

EMOTIONAL RESPONSE
THE ROOT OF EVIL

Have you noticed that you can solve everyone else's problem, but not your own? That is because emotion drives out understanding and common sense, replacing them with rationale. Knowledge and intellect are often substitutes for understanding and wisdom, just as pleasure is a substitute for happiness. Psychologists use the word "compensation" to describe the attempt to replace a spiritual emptiness with the nearest physical equivalent.

The feelings of fear and tension, and the desire to forget, draw to the alcoholic the idea, "If I had a drink, perhaps I would feel better." Later on, he says to himself, "Perhaps if I had another, I would feel better still." Smokers and excessive eaters are similar; they think with their feelings—their feelings cause them to think.

We all compensate for our "dis-ease" in millions of similar "iffing" ways. "If I had someone to love me…if I had lots of money…"

51

When we cannot give love, we need love. When we cannot understand, we need understanding. It is very frustrating,because no one has any to give us. We usually try to bring ourselves ease, relaxation and peace of mind through external or material endeavors, and that is impossible. These substitutes are not truly fulfilling, and only make us crave more of what does not fill; nothing really satisfies.

A person with a feeling of inferiority may seek an education in the secret hope that it will make him superior. He has rationalized that it's a lack of knowledge that makes him feel uncomfortable around people. Although he may gain much knowledge, he still has no understanding to use that knowledge.

The compulsive eater feels the same way, but he blames it all on his weight and thinks, "Perhaps if I could lose some of these pounds, I would feel more at ease." Often education, drinking, overeating and smoking are compulsive attempts to remove symptoms. The root of all our negative thinking lies in the emotions. The root of emotion lies in reaction to conditions.

For example: someone is rude to you. You react. You become angry—and your anger draws to it aggressive and negative thoughts; your thoughts in turn cause you to feel, do, or say things for which you are sorry later when the emotion is past.

In simpler terms, emotion gives rise to thoughts. You are driving down the highway and someone cuts in front of you. You think to yourself, "You stupid so-and-so, one of these days I'd like to buy an old fifty-dollar car and knock off your fenders!"

All kinds of daily irritations keep alive and revive unpleasant memories which should have been long forgotten. If

52

we dissolve the emotion, we no longer have that problem, and our negative thoughts, deprived of emotional support, begin to dissolve.

Nobody but you can overcome your problem. You have one because you allow people to trigger you emotionally, thereby giving their words and actions the power to direct you. You must learn to lead your own emotions. For the more you become emotionally upset, the less it takes to upset you the next time. The more you are influenced by the situation, the less you can lead yourself from the framework of reason. Tense, guilty and confused by your inability to control yourself or the situation, you resort to compensations and fall captive to compensatory illusions—your daydreams may become more real to you than the actual facts of the situation.

To rise above this weakness we need to do two things. First, we need to understand—just a little—because this understanding will grow with use; second, we must learn to relate emotionally by the light of understanding by detaching ourselves from the emotional influences of the cruelty and cunning of other people. If you have not found this self-relatedness, which manifests as self control, you cannot be objective to what you feel, what you think, or what you are.

For example, the dreamer feels as though he is falling in his sleep, because of what he thinks. He is not really falling, but he feels as though he is. He then reacts to what he feels by "catching himself" in his sleep. Surely we can feel guilt and fear in the same manner, because of what we continually rehearse in our minds towards others, this "thought stuff" having originated in our hostilities.

Another example: it is easy to make you angry by being rude, but if I told you beforehand that I was going to try this as an experiment, you would be mentally armed for the experience. Here we see that forewarning can prevent an emotional response. If we move into situations that normally upset us braced by a similar kind of mental preparation, the condition cannot affect us.

This attitude of alert preparedness that enables us to meet unexpected conditions gracefully also enables us to flow freely from one moment to the next, with no compulsion to look back. Because we have not become involved in the situation through emotional reaction (hostility, judgment, etc.), nothing of the situation "sticks" to us to draw us back into it or to distract us and render us unprepared for the next moment. It is therefore the active principle behind forgiveness.

To forgive means to forget. If you cannot forget, you cannot forgive. It is not what is forgotten that bothers you; it is what you compulsively remember. When you become annoyed, notice how you remember and rehearse unpleasant scenes in your mind. Through being upset, you have a good memory for the worthless things and a bad memory for the worthwhile.

The same pattern operates in people who experience great aggravation and become fearful of its happening again. The injustice stimulates anger, and the angry emotion gives rise to and nourishes repetitious thoughts, which in turn create the pattern and the anticipation of recurrence.

Observe also how emotion affects thought, and thought affects emotion. When we feel hungry, we think of food; but also when we think of food, we can feel hungry. When we become upset, we are caused to think. This negative thought in turn causes us to feel a secondary emotion, which produces foolish behavior that bypasses reason. This leads to guilt... then to the excuse. We become more irrational, and soon we are upset again. Now we feel bad, so we begin to worry. The

54

more we worry, the more we feel. The feeling affects our thoughts, the self-defeating cycle goes around and around—and anger turns the wheel.

Most of us cannot control ourselves, although we pretend to. We will labor "creatively" in order to work off tension and keep away from observing the source of our misery. We will wear ourselves out in order to feel tired enough to sleep. We may drown the morbid parade of thoughts by distractions, excitements, watching TV all day long or turning the radio on as loud as possible.

Because we cannot forgive, we may try to make up for our guilty feelings by bending over backwards to coerce people into liking us; then they merely take advantage and we are mad again.

Here we try to compensate for our inability to love, for as long as people are good, we can feel and think "good" toward others. We even boast about this terrible weakness. We will give in to avoid argument and upset, slowly giving up all our inner principles in the process, and then call ourselves "easygoing guys"; but we are still nervous volcanoes inside, now in conflict with ourselves instead of with others.

Usually a resentful person is one who conceals and suppresses his anger in various ways. To allow this hostility to build up until you have to let it out on another person is a great injustice to that person. Now you hurt him for the same reason other people hurt you: because you could not cancel your impatience and judgment with love.

Man without self-relatedness and understanding thinks without reason and control. What he feels like doing seems right, and what he does not feel like doing seems wrong. He is driven by selfmade fear, anxiety and excuses for his actions.

Fear and doubt indicate the absence of faith and draw

us into a pattern of anxiety. We no longer love to do what is right—we become pridefully afraid of making mistakes, which is not the same thing at all. Because of our decreasing understanding and failure to overcome our emotional response, we develop the increasing ability to compensate by analyzing and rationalizing, which we call worry.

The more we think into the past to find the answer to our problems, the more problems we create. The "if" goals we set up in our minds always fail to satisfy, and we become more confused than before. Therefore, the answer does not lie in external knowledge. That is why it cannot be found where we are presently looking.

The secret lies in understanding and self-relatedness, which are brought into view only by love of truth and the desire to move in obedience to basic spiritual principles. It is the emotional response of anger that announces our separation and fall from the bounds of reason and reveals our selfish pride and its relatedness to the call of error.

In psychoanalysis, the analysis is first and the direction is second. In meditation, understanding is first. Extended through the daily observation exercise, it gives our realization full power to change our behavior so that we need no longer be guilty before Truth (through being over-sensitive to life's experiences).

The Hebrew word for commandment literally means "to point the way" or "signpost." It implies that if one responds conscientiously to the instruction, it will lead him to more understanding and to an ultimate goal.

It is foolhardy to try to learn to swim while drowning. One would be wise to learn in shallow water in one's spare time. Likewise, if we are not interested enough to learn to control our reactions and emotions in our quiet moments, we

56

can hardly be prepared for emergencies.

The mental exercise you are acquiring accomplishes two things: first, we bring our thoughts and emotions under subjection; then we learn to relate back again to what is wise and true for each moment of living, while giving up our pride, judgment and desire for personal advantage. For example, instead of delighting in the stimulation of anger while observing another's cruelty or error, you remember the first principle of life: discerning patience. At the same moment, you undo your former bodily response to the situation, gaining a measure of correction and control from within yourself. With true patience and repentance, we can meet conditions that used to upset us with some claim to virtue and joy.

Your reaction on hearing this might be, "I do not get angry; I love everyone." But remember, just because you do not display your anger does not mean that you are not annoyed. Being overly nice to people could indicate that you are ashamed of that hostility—it becomes a subterfuge to compel people to love you so that they will not tempt you into displaying that hostility.

Basically, the second commandment of the New Testament says, "love thy neighbor as thyself." The way we feel towards others is the way we feel in ourselves. When you extend love, you feel the effect of goodness, but if you are resentful, your rebellion against right is reflected in getting angry with yourself.

The perfectionist is far from perfect; because of his need to judge, he cannot make allowances for others. He is wrong, and his impatience makes him more wrong—but that is painful to the perfectionist; so now he strives to offset that judgment by judging himself. Because he criticizes others, he feels self-criticism. Only through being patient with the faults of others can we eliminate our own errors. Hostility and judgment are products of faults. Patience and forgiveness are the opposite in effect; they are fault-reducers. So if you can say, "I have no faults," then you can also say, "I have no resentment (judgment)."

No thought is lasting, whether it be positive or negative. It must have emotional energy to keep it alive. Negative, morbid thoughts are created and kept alive through the daily feeding of irritation. The nervous businessman may take a trip to leave the source of his aggravation behind. Soon he begins to feel better, but when he returns, things are more depressing than ever. Granted, getting away from the problem helps temporarily, but the real and permanent solution lies in learning to be calm in the face of all that besets us.

The meditation exercise keeps alive our inward rapport with reality by creating emotional response to the world within rather than the world without. It teaches us to respond more and more to our own understanding, to what we know is wise, and less and less to crutches, remedies and the temptations of wicked people. We discover through meditation that we need not depend on external conditions to be good, healthy, or happy. We can be healthy, successful and happy most of the time in spite of the situation. We are not controlled by the situation. We influence life through not being influenced by adversity and temptation—we wield the influence of no influence by responding with non-response. We love by not hating.

The meditation exercise destroys the angry response, which is the cause of most of our negative thinking. The person who returns anger for anger becomes part of the evolution of cruelty in the conspiracy of evil. Anyone can be kind to those who are kind to him. But this ability doesn't make us

58

right or good—just easily led by scoundrels who can control our moods through their "kindness." As long as you act only as you are "moved to" by the situation outside, you cannot be individual in your thinking—you cannot think properly unless conditions are good.

You could spend your entire lifetime devising ways to make people like you; but you would win the admiration of fools, thereby losing the "persecution for righteousness' sake" that enables you to bear witness to truth and makes you strong and virtuous.

Before each lesson, listen and take special note of the following. You may not understand now, but tomorrow or the next day you will. Animals respond to danger in one of two ways: they run, or they fight. When we become annoyed or irritated by some trivial thing and say or do nothing, we create an accumulating pressure to run (in animal ways). This is called fear, a wrong response from a human viewpoint. Because we do not know why we feel this way, we may seek to identify it with something in order to remedy it. That is why we are often afraid of many things without apparent reasons, like storms, driving a car, failure of any kind, crowds—especially crowds, because it was people who caused the anger in the beginning.

Most guilt feelings are compulsively compounded. Your anger makes you wrong. You start thinking of little retaliations towards those who wrong you from day to day—like what you should have said, what you might have done. Your thoughts make you feel more guilty, just like the sleeping man can feel as though he is falling again and again in his dreams. Now, to escape your present shame, perhaps you search into your past to find out what makes you feel this way—and then you find the wrong reason. Now you try to change the past— more error, more angry frustration. You either cannot forgive

59

yourself, or you blame someone else unfairly, which gives you a reason to be irritated and to judge again, which in turn makes you feel more guilty. While trying to change your past and plan your future, you fail again in the present.

Guilt can be falsely identified in thousands of subtle ways. For example: "I feel guilty for not doing more for my children (or my husband or wife before he or she passed away)...for being unable to pay my debts...for not being able to work more...I feel guilty about sex, how I treated my mother and father, etc...." Individuals who feel this way may seek to compensate for guilt. They will give everything to their children (as a claim to virtue) and will not discipline them. They cannot say "no" to requests, and they spend all their time seeking approval from other people—giving all kinds of assistance to the wrong people, instead of living rightly in the presence of their own families and those who really need them. We all seek to reinstate a feeling of righteousness in ourselves by appearing right in the eyes of strangers when we have responded unjustly to our own family.

Resentment and anger can create an act of suppression which eventually becomes a conditioned reflex. Sooner or later, we are kept so busy suppressing our wrong reactions that we are unable to express truth for each moment. Hostility continues to sweep away sensible opposition with a flood of emotion, which we dare not express. So we say nothing, walk away, or cry. On occasion, we blow up, as we can no longer control ourselves. When the point is reached when we are completely absorbed in the full-time preoccupation of suppression, we shall have to push ourselves to work. Without inner motivation and natural expressiveness, the mind is a maze of excuses. We cannot see truth, so we find it difficult to make decisions for ourselves. We now depend on others. In our insecurity we develop a need for people, which we foolishly call love. When they advise us well, we depend on them, but if they make mistakes we resent them. This resentment adds momentum to the cycle of angry emotion.

Because of our dependency upon the prod of environment, we procrastinate. We move only when we are upset, but that is the wrong time. We worry about what we have not done and resent what we must do, which grows increasingly difficult. Now we worry because we are afraid of making another mistake. Or we seek a reason to motivate us or excuse our inactivity. Now we have more to do and less time to do it—more worry!

We will sit daydreaming—changing the past error and offsetting future mistakes—to avoid seeing our weakness in the present. With hundreds of things in our minds we may read a whole page of the newspaper and not know a single word of it when we are finished. We follow the writing only with our eyes, but not our understanding. (By the way, this is one reason that disturbed children fail in school.)

Each time we allow ourselves to become annoyed, we must follow through with a chain reaction of emotionalized thought, word and deed, and each day our life becomes more negative.

Resentment is the father of our complexities and confusion.

Positive thinking and well-being is a present you cannot give yourself. It comes as a gift from God—for remembering each moment to make allowances for your fellow man.

4

Meditation as a Power for Good
The Influence of not Being Influenced
The Stress of Non-Response to Stress

Each time we allow ourselves to react emotionally to pressures, it takes a little less pressure to cause us to respond with more violence or more unbearable repression...until small irritations can make us explode or make us withdraw until we become insensitive to feeling. Progressively, we lose our grip over our mind and body, becoming conditioned and molded by outer demands.

Our only alternatives are: 1) to become upset and hurt others, or 2) to become upset and repress that emotion to the detriment of our own health and well-being.

Animals were ordained to react to circumstances. The adaptations resulting from their reactions bring about changes in them. The process is known as evolution. It is natural for each creature to respond to and take its cue from its environment.

But we, as human beings, have no tolerance for evolutionary pressures. Circumstance was not meant to be our master. We need to unfold from a higher order of purpose.

Certain reactions which bypass the modifying influence of reason cause us to compensate—compel us to take our development from an alien intelligence behind the pressures. Responding emotionally, we allow the source of our development to shift from the inside to the outside. When we fall to the process of evolution, it becomes, for us, devolution, degeneration and disease. Something hideous takes shape within, which at first we may not want to see.

Because animals adapt to the stimulation of their environment, environment is their master. If there is no pressure other than environment, what hope have we? Fortunately, there is another pressure. It is called conscience.

When we allow ourselves to become upset, we become subjects of mischievous influence. Responding to conditions with undue emotion, we gradually lose sight of all reason and control over our body functions, which then become governed by the stress, mood, or feeling arising from unfriendly influences. Becoming more and more sensitive in this process, we are unable to change the world for good. The invisible forces mold us negatively. Changes cause guilt and fear. The light of understanding may cause you to become aware of a malevolent intelligence, which can lead you only if you are upset, excited or frightened.

The meditation has revealed to you the principle for meeting any excitement correctly. However, observing our need to dissolve emotional responses to the outside is only the beginning. We must also not become upset with what appears in ourselves.

By resigning to an inner pressure, responding and taking shape from an intuitive impulse each moment, we take on a new nature and become creators of stress. Being a vehicle of a new order of life, you will cause others to feel a pressure upon them, which compels them to respond, but only because of your non-response. While they are externally turned on and sensitive to pressure, you are not.

By your witness of what is right, you unknowingly compel their energy-sensitive bodies to live according to what is sensible. Egocentrically, they will not want to do so, but they will have no choice—just as you were committed according to their guile when you had no control.

Because of fear due to growing emotional sensitivity to severe pressures, delinquents and malcontents develop a ruthless need to cause others to respond emotionally to them, thus regaining a sense of courage and power they had lost through having yielded to bigger monsters in their own lives. Becoming a threat, they momentarily feel less threatened. In other words, they become the source of fear in others in order to minimize their own fears, which were caused by their reactions to similar brutalities inflicted upon them. They display a relative courage, a type of superiority derived at the expense of others. They soon become dependent upon the anger, fear and reaction of their victims for this sense of value.

I am not suggesting that we influence people in this fashion; I am showing a way of conquering your fears and inferiorities and affecting people simply through not being affected by their need to pressure and impress you. This will, incidentally, discourage bullies and stand as a correction to them.

First, we are patient. Patience may itself be sufficient activity. Then, if we are prudent, we will see clearly to speak and act from an emotionally undistorted view of the situation.

Through the meditation exercise, we influence simply by not being influenced—discern by not judging—love by not resenting. We cause response simply by not responding…we obtain by not coveting…and own by not seeking to possess. We stand as evidence of what is correct by our ability to hold sway over our emotions. Others, feeling our calm observations of them as they really are, are caused to feel exposed.

The key lesson includes this directive that leads to higher awareness: be plain-spoken—with firmness, kindness and patience. Whatever you have to say, say it. Whatever you have to do, do it. The reminder to "overlook" simply means, do not become resentful over the overt or secret intents of others. Detect and observe them without being emotionally swayed or excited to judge. As long as your impulse to speak or act does not arise from anger or flattery, and you have no malice, you have every right to express yourself. Wise men will find value in your rebuke and they will respect you. Your enemies will be exposed and disarmed.

Naturally, by discerning the nature of the error, you are creating newer stress upon yourself. You are evincing the truth as it is revealed from within each moment. You are moving without guile, speaking plainly, disregarding consequence, not carefully planning to your advantage—but you will experience persecution. Your body will begin to feel the pressure that again will reveal unseen weakness and show you the need for patience, which is then extended to you via meditation.

Before we learned the meditation exercise, we responded in a vicious cycle to troubles that we emotionally perpetuated. Now we are simply getting back what we deserved and did not graciously bear in the past. Now a virtuous cycle is set in motion through the opposition we create because of our principles. We are persecuted for our right, not our wrong. The pattern of truth is progressively and unerringly brought

66

forth by the opposition to our witness.

The first opposition comes when we first glimpse reality. A little light is shining. Our adversary sees it as a threat and attacks. Our reply to that attack is the next threat to the error that is moving up through our adversary and he counterattacks. So it progresses. We must patiently bear what we cannot change in this matter—without fear or resentment.

Patience is the reaction of what is right in us. It is felt by others as a power to see through guile, as a deterrent and correction instead of a support for their egocentric, selfish intents. It may be their first experience with such devastating resistance.

People take their cue from a feedback due to your response to them, and they depend upon your reaction for their next move and their sense of rightness. But when you do not respond, they are alarmed and disarmed. Furthermore, they see you observing them and will feel threatened, fearful, or even furious.

Although "democratic" people declare that each person has a right to live his own life, they are constantly contradicting themselves. They are extremely intolerant. They dare not let you live the right way, because egocentrically they demand temptation to keep them free from what you inwardly embrace! They do not desire the correction you offer. It is agony to them. Hold fast. Remain calm. They will resort to the principle of flattery. Still hold fast. Do not be blinded or excited by compliments, because you have discovered that excitement to pride is the root of error.

An animal's development is supported emotionally. For animals, that is normal, part of the natural growth process. When we respond in this way, our mind darkens and our flesh thickens like the beast's as we are led emotionally down from reason. That is how we become controlled. Pride needs emotion to spark selfish activity and forgetfulness of conscience, to uphold its way and its image of righteousness.

Each time we are excited or disturbed, we progress a little further in the development of beastly lust, sickness, fear, conflict and frustration. Unfortunately, until we find the original fount of life within, we need those pressures, although we have no real tolerance for them.

As the beast survives only as long as it stands separate from the enemy's belly by virtue of strength, so shall we live successfully only as we stand firm in our denial of temptation. When upsets get under our skin, they alter our nature, and we become obliged to test others for their weakness, so that they too might fall, or grow.

The danger lies in the petty, unjust threats that ambitious, unreasonable people provide to lead you down from your center of calmness. If you respond, you will become like them.

What disables us from dealing with natural conditions wisely is our response to flattery, praise, or criticism. This leads us away from dealing with problems with the modifying factor of an enlightened reason, so that we are always resentful, growing as a reply to provocation, as do the animals, except that, in our case, evil holds the pattern of growth, instead of nature.

Although temptation has been our downfall, it is also important for our regeneration. It is as though you had learned to play the piano incorrectly, and someone took away the piano. You could never hope to improve or to become an accomplished pianist until you obtained another piano and practiced the correct methods.

If you become numb, withdrawn from your surroundings, you cannot change for the better. You will be without experience to correct the fault. However, before facing each new day, we must be sure to meditate in order to meet life correctly and touch others with the virtues of patience. Otherwise we perpetuate the evolution of trouble.

Protecting our children from temptation is not to be confused with living their lives for them, which does great harm. With love, we shield them from wrong involvements with others until they come to see their way clearly and are strong enough to follow their conscience in spite of temptation.

Overconcern conveys to a child that he is an asset of positive or negative value to you. One kind of concern, criticism, offends his vanity and makes him resentful. Excessive praise, on the other hand, fills him with false self-esteem. Resentful, or intoxicated with pride, he cannot discern clearly to deal with life. And so we parents *produce* the problem we fear.

The resentful, pressured, over-protected child will often seek trouble in which to grow. He is drawn to the very troubles his parents fear (in the name of love). In his rebellion, he deliberately creates trouble as a challenge for growth, and in so doing, actually seizes the bait (the hidden temptation implicit in the parent's concern). Alas! His resentment disables him from dealing with the problems he created, so the child adds fuel to the fears of the rescuing parents whom he hates.

You are often tempted to try to alter the mistakes you have produced in those you claim to love, but you must cease your efforts to rescue the image of yourself in the guise of helping and loving them. You need to desist from your compulsive meddling and get off their backs, thus allowing pressure from within themselves to correct your loved ones.

We must learn to discipline without bribery or fear. We must impress our children with the strength of patience, perceive their faults without judgment (anger), and provide firm, good, calm direction. Just by living rightly, we become a subtle pressure. Through love's enforced requirements, we keep them separate from too much socializing until they become mature enough to choose wisely from the alternatives that are clear to their unruffled observation. Thus they are not blinded by the excitements of the unfolding process of error and excuses invoked by a world that "loves" these children of yours into becoming one of its own—loves them as a lion loves his prey.

While we must regret the harm we have done to our children in the past, we need only concern ourselves with living rightly now. Then our confused children will challenge our new light, and here we will have our second chance to meet them with love. Thus the past will be repaired in the present.

It has been the emotional response to challenge that has caused our internal strife, and our vain attempts to deal with the ensuing problems with force, impatience and anger which have caused still greater confusion.

We must realize that the old emotional responses could never have been possible were we always inclined toward bringing forth what was fair for each moment. Instead, we were preoccupied with personal ambition and glory—too busy worrying, making money, being a success—needing love and emotion to bring about our heart's desire and to adjust our failing image, projecting our problems upon others to minimize their presence in us.

Emotional non-response to pressures has great spiritual significance. Non-response is a response, but not to the cunning pressure. Patient non-response cancels out the effect of conditioning. When we are turned on from within, we are turned off from the programming of the world.

Conditioned reflex has made us more and more mechanical and led us away from reason and independence. Patience (non-response) will starve our egocentric will by depriving it of the daily-dose nourishment of emotionality that has promoted its growth. One by one, our sins will emerge from the body as babble thoughts, to be observed and resolved in the light of understanding.

The lessening of ego need (desire for power, wealth and glory) strips temptation of its power. The non-response to things is synonymous with response (change, unfolding and development) to the true source of life. It opens up a whole new inexpressible world of psychology. Each time we are patient we starve the roots of the old way. When the emotional roots wither, negative thought patterns lose their power to obscure or stand in the light of reason.

So our minds are remolded from within. We grow out of a different order. Count it a joy when you now meet pressure and temptation. Without upsetting conditions, we have nothing on which to practice our new way. The trying of our insight works patience. Let patience make every work perfect.

The claim to virtue is in the face of temptation, without which we would be obliged to remain a temptation ourselves. So you see, even the bad will work to our ultimate good, if our desire is toward that good and we prove it by denying temptation. Withdrawing from experience (to save face) is a foolish mistake, for by withdrawing (saving ourselves) we elude the gift of salvation.

Observing what we have become, without hiding, excusing or being angry with it—feeling our utter helplessness—refines into the pain called repentance, which brings a reply of new growth. Step by step, pain turns to joy, defeat to victory, despair to hope. This helplessness (not hopelessness) and pain, humility, stresses the Spirit to compassion and provides a remedy that will strengthen your wonder (faith).

Without meditation, you cannot live with your problems. Neither can you live without them.

Once upon a time, when you escaped from what disturbed you, there appeared in you a conscience concerning the way you had handled the situation. Egotistically, you returned to the situation in order to make amends for what you had done, or not done—not to do right, but to repair your damaged image. Because your motive was wrong, you again failed to relate to the moment correctly, thus causing bigger arguments and resentments. Heretofore, you have not been armed with the mystical essence acquired through right intent implemented by meditation.

Armed with a desire to face reality, we shall see our wrong motives and faulty responses. The pain of this seeing stresses the power of love to come through us, to correct our shortcomings and to stand as evidence of good to others.

The brain of man is designed to serve the conscious will. Our will should in turn desire to be overshadowed by a divine purpose.

In metaphysical language, the entire body should live in subjection to the consciousness. Just as a well-trained athlete keenly awaits the signal that will set him in motion, so should the body attend the consciousness.

Selfish, proud, unaware, then excited and upset, we allow temptation to lead our attention captive, and our body is pulled away from its preordained purpose. The less we modify our emotions and reactions, the less we can modify them. Struggling like a man in a swamp, we are left to our own insufficient devices. So we are led into captivity by

72

what we respond to—whether it be "for" or "against." We are shaped by what stimulates us. By responding to the praise of evil people we become evil.

The object of the meditation exercise is to free you from your squirrel cage by bringing the unconscious into subjection to the consciousness. This is made possible only through desiring guidance of an invisible Divine Will that we may know, or come to know, only as conscience. Hence, we must dissolve all mental chatter in our mind, and fast from the excitement of "love" and hate that propels our selfish pride in its striving toward selfish goals. We must wait, empty, for a new direction.

We were designed to be intuitively impelled. Without this, we are ships without rudders, at the mercy of everyone's opinions and selfish motives. The animal has no conscious awareness. Its instinctive (parallel, but not equal to, intuitive) responses lead it to food and water—and survival.

Our egocentric needs alienate us from a higher order of relatedness, so we find ourselves responding to the same pressures to which others have fallen. When we respond with excitement and anger, we are bound to an invisible enemy. The rebel and the conformist are equally his subjects, and the result is accumulating tension and fear.

If we become angry and try to prevail, we are evolving in his system. We then become more vicious than those who served us so unjustly, and it is not long before we become just like them—enabling them to hide their faults behind our greater fault—greater because of what we have become as the result of our response.

Responding emotionally, we cannot live a good, true or useful life. We are dominated by the wickedness of others—whose wickedness we shall come to need to provide the energy for our rebellious "independence" and for the sense of rightness that arises from judging their wickedness. We now find that we are unkind to those we would "love" to love. We take out our resentments on them and make them worse. If we yield to pressure to avoid seeing the growth of violence within, we are aiding the enemy and standing in silent support of wickedness.

We may find ourselves hypnotically attracted by danger and trouble, often feeling the subconscious desire to yield because of our tendency to conform to pressures of a spiritual nature. Typical of this is the compulsion to throw oneself off a high building.

Confusion and hostility are rarely triggered by true kindness. They are usually sired by our response to someone's malicious intent, whether it be expressed in the form of needling us into rash judgment or in the form of sticky sweetness.

If we went back far enough into the past, we would discover that the injustice of the persons we resent was relayed to them by their reactions of hatred toward preceding generations. If you take out your resentment on your family, you then become the tempter. We must surely see that it takes real courage and strength to be patient. Any fool can be excited—and all fools are!

To live unto God we must accept the essence of grace to enable us to gaze unflinchingly into the face of our tempters and tormentors, unaffected by their flattery or criticism. We must not be threatened by wickedness, nor should we covet apparent advantages or superiority.

Without love, we become dependent upon impatience, anger and excitement as energizers. We do not speak out until we are irritated or excited. And of course this is always the wrong time. If you do not play back the emotional advances of others, a strange thing happens. They feel guilty because, meeting one who has no need for excitement, they see their own motive for what it was. The contrast between your patience and their wrong intent shames them for having forced themselves on you. On the other hand, if you fall for temptation or return hostility, you encourage your tormentors to advance, and enable them to justify their wrong. In the end, they are actually tormented by your failure to reprimand them in a proper way.

Your emotional responses serve the cause of error in the world. However, if you stand firm and do not respond with emotion, you evince love, which removes the catalyst for further mischief. If you have ever resented someone who turned out to be kind after all, you will understand this principle.

When confronted with real virtue, people feel uneasy. Your patient presence reminds them of what they wish to forget. They may bend over backwards to please, in order to confuse you as to their secret motive—try to outclass you with "goodness" to make you feel guilty. They constantly test you, probing for the guilt of pride and judgment and the need to be glorified. This is a subtle game. Careful! If you are correct, you will not be toppled by praise or tricked by guile.

When you react with anger, fear, guilt and pride, you provide those to whom you are reacting with justification for what they are, and empower them to continue in their ways. If you applaud their "kindness," you license them for more mischief. You may do so to relieve the guilt you feel for having judged them, or because you have begun to enjoy their kingly treatment of you, never realizing that they have conned you into the position of freeing them from the stigma of their guilt. People will not repent of their cunning ways as long as you provide them with justification, either through being more wrong than they are, or through letting them manipulate you into approving them as they are.

If I am upset with my child, I become the uglier extension of his mood, which in turn energizes him to judge me. But if I direct him calmly, with firmness, kindness and patience (which still might irritate him), he will soon begin to feel truly guilty. He may soon put his little arms around me, which means he is sorry. He may start doing little chores without my asking. (Now I must be careful not to give approval for what is naturally right to do. A person who lives rightly doesn't need any praise.) This kind of guilt and remorse is the beginning of true repentance, which leads our children to salvation and natural love, and we shall have become their subtle guides.

Of course, another kind of guilt can arise in our children by reason of their resentment of our false kindness or capricious treatment of them (angry one minute, nice the next). This causes a guilt in them that is relative to us instead of to their own conscience in secret, and they find themselves committed to resolving the guilt in the wrong way, through agonized laboring for our approval.

Science has proved that emotion adversely affects our bodily metabolism. Response means change. However, any alteration of our nature should be the result of responding to the inside, not reacting to the outside.

When we become angry or frightened, certain glands are stimulated to prepare our body to meet the threat by changing its chemistry. You might say, "Surely this is normal!" I would reply, "Yes, it is, but only to resolve the problems of natural stress." Even then, if the action we take is to be truly human, it must have its roots in reason and not in emotions. It should be

76

markedly different from the unmodified emotional response of the growing animal. Through our egocentric need for excitement and resentment, our conscience is loosened from the soil of reason, weakened to become unduly affected by nature in an animal-like way. Our mind darkens; our flesh becomes brutish.

When we allow ourselves to be led down from reason by temptation, we set off metabolic changes in our bodies that lead to degeneration and the arousing of animal lusts. We may grow afraid to meet new situations because of their effect upon our nature, for once we have forsaken the way of reason, the indiscretion of our lusts causes us to become involved with the wrong people who allow us to express our lust without shame. The release from shame whets our desires even more. And so it goes until we are pock-marked by pressure. Instead of bringing forth good, we become herded and programmed like evolving beasts. Our rundown condition invites disease. Yet the proud mind adjusts to each change and justifies and defends it with anger. In its newer but more degenerate state, it is still more susceptible to the call of temptation.

We fight our sickness with the same energy of anger. As our soul becomes subject to temptation, our body becomes subject to disease. Paradoxically, our only immunity is to drugs and to the truth. Through uncontrolled fear, the clotting level of our blood falls to dangerous extremes. We begin to smoke, drink and take pills—then more pills to cancel out the effect of pills—all to make us feel better without being better as persons. Solutions beget problems endlessly.

We cannot accept responsibility for foolish decisions and failures, so we seek advice from people who lead us further away from functioning from our higher self, which in turn leads to greater confusion. We cherish the weakness that led to our original fall, secretly reserving the right to blame the temptation when the chips are down.

Learn to stand up under cruelty without resentment. If you accomplish this, after the real stress has passed, your entire nature is strengthened by your experience and others will be glad that you remained calm. But if we meet life with anger, jealousy, hate, hostility and hurt feelings, our guilt will grow with the years. Worsening, we become angry with ourselves and our sickness. We try to force ourselves to be well. This adds error to error and inflames our plight.

So dependent are we on outside stimulation that very often we can't move a muscle until someone burns the toast. We marry for the emotional drive our spouses foster in us by their unreasonable ways, their pressure and support. Our hatred provides the drive in the form of a sense of right-ness and a wicked strength. Egotists don't want to lose their reason for hostility for fear of losing their "success drive." Unconsciously, we often seek a spouse to take the position formerly occupied by a parent. We continue to need someone to resent, to feel right about what we became by resenting. It is a way of life!

Hating wrong, we are more wrong, and we become dependent upon hating in order to feel right about what we became by hating! We have never known how to function without emotion.

We may one day become conscious that emotion is killing us and flee from all pressure into an unhealthy repose. When we begin to realize that we have become slaves of a conditioning process that was set in motion by our reactions to temptation, we come face to face with a terrible dilemma. The only life stimulus we know is excitement, yet with it we grow wrongly—and without it, we rot. To find a right way of life, we must find a right life-stimulus. That is why we need to meditate.

Meditation establishes a new relationship. Energy becomes available from within, so that we no longer have to wait for fear, irritation or temptation to move us. What we do, say and think is intuitively impelled and friction-free. We grow in a new way—to see more and to respond more to what we perceive. Naturally, without effort, we are impelled to do what we realize is wise and to shrink from what is unwise. In this way we come to rule our own bodies and escape from our old enslavement to pleasure and pain.

Our unreasonable responses to the unpleasant and pleasant have produced guilt in us, and we have made the mistake of trying to resolve the guilt by distractions: new excitements, a change of scene, a new hat. But these distractions have only increased our inner turmoil. We just can't erase our bad feelings by covering them up with good feelings, for the only truly happy state of being lies in subservience to conscience. Pleasure, in the form of distractions and comforts, only precludes the correcting factor (conscience) and leads to greater conflict and sickness.

The pursuit of comfort or pleasure is an escape from the correcting factor of conscience—a movement away from what is truly healing. This kind of escape merely generates bigger problems. In a sense, it is self-perpetuating in that it continues to provide us with a growing pain, a greater need to escape.

When we fail to obtain glory, success, happiness and contentment by means of our pleasures and egocentric pursuits, we are frustrated. This sharpens our bodily sensitivity to pleasure and pain. If we continue, we may eventually become afraid of the pain that pleasure, worldly success and wrong decisions bring us, and so become frozen into inactivity—impotent and frigid. In the meanwhile, those who promote distraction are addicted to our needs and hooked on the same excitement we are. They know that pleasure promotes guilt and conscious pain, and that soon we will be back for another shot.

The meditation exercise is the key to withstanding the evil pressures that are bound to challenge you as you grow to meet them. It will strengthen the rapport between the inner self and the outer self, so that you will touch each moment and everything you do with discretion and love.

Be watchful for temptation in your imagination, such as "You feel better now; you don't need to meditate." You may actually hear voices dissuading you from the good life. They appeal to your ego-reason. They try to frighten and persuade. At these moments, call upon His name silently and you will be saved from the evil. Don't panic. You must learn to be aware at all times. You may awaken occasionally from sleep, feeling pressure. Meditate at these times and rest again. Never allow material pursuits to overshadow or become more important than your inner attentiveness to reality.

Usually there is a little reluctance to meditate. Do not let your thoughts tell you to wait until you feel like doing the meditation; if you do, you will fall into another trap. The whole purpose of the exercise is to command both feeling and thought.

Whatever problem you wish to resolve, be careful you do not worry about its achievement. If you do, you will not be able to keep your mind properly focused. Your concern is with the root of the problem, not its surface effect. You must dissolve all distracting mental activity, including worry and analysis. Excuses and mental garbage must be dispelled. It is a daily battle, but only as the veil of mental chatter is pierced and you become quiet, can you see each layer of the problem unpeeling to expose its hidden seed in the light of reality.

The meditation exercise represents a commitment to a true way of life. It must remain a choice, and never become an obligation. It will never become a compulsive ritual as long as it represents your daily free-will choice between two ways. Incidentally, don't be surprised when you discover that the practice of meditation with a true intent will cause a good way of life to appear over which you will have no control. You will simply become a vehicle for the ultimate good…just as you were before for what was not good.

It is the divine hypnosis. The same process that created compulsions from the outside corrects those compulsions when it is inwardly directed. You will not immediately see that Intelligence, except through manifestation. First, you will see truth vaguely, then more clearly, then face-to-face. As it was in error, so it is in truth.

Our former existence was one of enslavement due to those responses that trapped us between two wrong alternatives. We say we love our way of life, or that we love others, in order to hide from admitting our addiction, dependency, enslavement.

The voices you hear are straight from Hades. They have been guiding you to your present dilemma, but you believed them to be originating within yourself. You may be getting the old pitch: "You deserve better than this…what are you suffering for?" The voices may exhort you to do away with yourself, promising rest and peace. They have always lied. Follow those voices no more. You believed them only because your pride could not accept the truth.

Reality does not speak aloud, but it shines a light on every error and shows the disparity between the familiar wrong and the unknown right. It is a gentle pressure moving you from evil to good.

The meditation exercise will be the only nonhabit-forming "habit" you can acquire. There is no compulsion to do it. However, should you stop, you will have exercised your choice to allow the old way of life to take over again.

There is but one true repentance. As you grow in consciousness, you may see clearly what you are required to give up. At that moment, you stand upon the threshold of eternal life or death.

After you have become thoroughly familiar with the meditation exercise, you may be moved to accomplish it in other positions—lying down, sitting, or even kneeling. The hands may be clasped together in a prayer-like fashion, but however you hold them, it is imperative that you concentrate on them as you have been shown. Be aware of your hands. Feel them tingle as the life flows into them. Be aware of the place in the middle of your forehead, as though you are looking out through it into space. Feel the awareness of your hands, and then go back again to the awareness of the middle of your forehead. It is as though you were extending a conscious awareness of the present and what it contains to touch every fiber of your being, by concentrating upon the tingling of your fingers. Keep doing it.

Once you have clearly understood the sheer beauty of this simple meditation, you will be able to accomplish it alone. But be sure not to add any kind of affirmation or suggestion. Just be still, and you will come to know and grow. Your true desire should be to have a quiet soul, from which vantage you will see yourself and your thoughts and how they originate, by the light of reality. The first truth you will see is the truth about your own errors and the errors of others. Wait now…

watch your thoughts and memories as they come into your mind. The wrong deeds you once believed to be right will pain your conscience, for you both allowed them and justified them. Seeing them again will bring a pain called guilt.

Good! Don't be upset. Bear the discomfort without trying to remedy it. Know that you cannot change what you have become in the past. Be sorry. Desire to be better. It was the selfish, blaming, excuse-making, lie-loving, easily-deceived pride that allowed the problem to grow up in you. It was being angry at everything that got in your way that made matters still worse—as if pride, aided by anger and fear, could solve problems! It was the egocentric struggle to ease or escape the pain of conscience that prevented the true pain from becoming a correction. It was fighting evil with the illusion that it made you good to do so, that actually made you worse.

First there was conflict. But in excusing yourself and trying to rid yourself of blame, you gave power to the lie. Then it became the truth to you.

Then came confusion. You may come back the way you came—from confusion to conflict. If this is so, good! Don't worry or become upset. Being excited is never conducive to handling problems, inside or out.

See your part of the mistake. Be truly sorry. Acknowledge your own lack. Wait without impatience. What you may receive as a gift of life, you do not deserve. Long to be a better person, knowing that of yourself you have no power over evil, nor can you change the color of one hair on your head. Put aside all thoughts of advantage, glory, love, affection, riches and pride-power.

Dispel the mist of excuses. Quieten the mental chatter; then observe your own errors as they appear, without excusing them. Allow the pain of conscience to loom up to overshadow you and redeem you progressively from your faults. Be patient.

The pain you will feel is repentance. Bear it for a while without cursing it or dealing with it; just watch it, perhaps with tears of regret. Soon it will pass. Soon things will become new again—not because I say so, but because that is the way it will be, by the grace of God. Your change of heart is the beginning of great wisdom. It is the pain of error and the knowledge of one's own lack that stresses the compassion of the Spirit within. This is all we can do for salvation— observe, know, repent, and wait for the next opportunity to do right what we once did wrong.

Watch your thoughts rise to the surface, peeling off one by one…creating the discomfort of repentance. This stresses the compassion of the Father, if no other remedy is sought.

Your conscience, pained by your variance with reality, will be assuaged as you yield and are overshadowed by that inner pressure. Then there will come warmth and rest. Conflict will ease.

Each time you do the exercise, you will be responding less and less to unjust pressures around you, especially the things people imply in those petty, mean digs they give you to hurt your feelings. Then, not being offended emotionally, you are not impressed by their suggestions. They will roll off you like water off a duck's back. You will no longer be proud, so you need not feel threatened by negative remarks and unkindness. You can switch off the hostility and emotional, angry defenses. You may feel external pressure upon you, but it will stay outside your skin.

You should look upon irrational behavior as a kind father looks on naughty children—emotionally detached, unmoved, and yet compassionate—concerned, where compassion is fitting, but not worried. This is the way you should react in any situation that involves the unkind actions of others. Be careful not to seize upon any subtle cruelty to puff you up to judgment and self-righteousness. Correction of others, when necessary, must be done without emotion—forcefully perhaps, and at the moment it is needed. Don't wait to get upset!

You must overlook, right on the spot. This means you must not respond with resentment when these things happen. You must also overlook praise when its aim is to tempt you, to excite and exalt your pride. It's only the other side of the coin. Both criticism and praise can be used to fatten us for the kill, but only if we respond.

Each time you overcome your irritability, you are increasing your response to a gentle intuitive pressure. Not because I say so, but because it is so. This pressure will make you aware of any discrepancy in the behavior of others. Perhaps you will not fully understand the reasons behind those discrepancies…you will just observe and be guided by your intuitive perception in such relationships. Each time you face the small issues of life this way, it will become easier to face bigger ones. Again, not because I say so, but because it is self-evident. If you remember to do this, you will find yourself becoming more stable under greater amounts of stress, until what you thought was stress will cease to be stress at all.

When you are patient, it is easier to speak out from your clear perception, to say what is wise and sensible. You will be able to speak what you know is right, and you will not be concerned with the outcome, or the way other people react to your words. You have the courage to speak truly, regardless of advantages or disadvantages.

As long as you do not have the intention of elevating

yourself or hurting anyone with your words, you have every right to speak up. Your friends will respect you for it, and others will hear what they need to hear. They must be pained by truth; otherwise, they cannot come to repent. Because you will be outspoken with firmness, kindness and patience, other people will begin to react to the reason in you. If you create a disturbance at times, because of your outspokenness, and people become angry, you will have more reason to be patient, and you will become stronger in the practice of patience.

This is the best kind of stress, because you have set it in motion through your embrace of what is fair and true, through having put aside all thought of ambition or consequence in favor of seeing justice prevail. A little anxiety in anticipation of a stressful situation is normal enough, as long as you are not angry, annoyed, irritated or impatient. You will be strengthened by difficult conditions, and each experience will prepare you to face greater tests to come.

With your ego out of the way, the Spirit of Truth will reply for you. Do not give up principles for any material gain or credit, for anything you might gain in that way will eventually take possession of you. Be patient, seek first what is right, and all things will come to you as a matter of course. Virtue is your greatest asset.

All of your possessions must work for you. You are not supposed to labor for them. If you labor for things you cannot afford, merely to give your ego a lift, you will be enslaved by these things. At best, you will feel guilty for all your vain striving, unable even to enjoy rest. When we buy new clothes, a car or a house for prestige, we are using material things to provide emotional support for our egos.

Here we tend to gain a sense of rightness that is not right at all, but which increases the hunger for greater amounts of material support. Therefore,do not try to fill up your lack with material things; do not hunger for them. Seek first the goodness of God and the path of life He would have you take. Put truth and righteousness for each moment first, and all other things shall follow in due course. Material things will then work for you, and all things will work together for good. Then you will feel no shame for not having, nor guilt for having.

Do not seek the approval of other people. If people like you, that does not make you good or right. On the contrary, if you labor for the approval of others, you are merely trying to compensate for your failure to live rightly each moment. That labor for approval, and the receiving of that approval, only makes you more wrong. Your labor to this end is a waste of life substance—an added motion away from the real purpose prepared for you.

As long as you honestly seek the truth and desire to do what is just for each moment—as long as you desire to bear witness to good, without trying to *be* that good or to take credit for good deeds or wisdom, you will always be able to see what is right for each moment. You will not fall. When you overcome irritation, you can do what you perceive to be fair from a center of calmness. You will not feel the need of approval from other people, nor will you have an emotional need to condemn.

If you become more perceptive and joyful than others, you will invariably find that some people will feel uncomfortable around you, but it is only because you possess a quality they don't want to see. This may make some of them cruel, resentful and jealous. They will call you crazy or cold. Do not believe them. Do not concern yourself about the way other people feel, as you cannot help the way they feel. You are not responsible for their follies. If they insist on being unwise, it is better for them to suffer than it is for you to give up your principles to comfort them and protect them from their pain.

Some people are always trying to make you conform to their way of thinking. They seek relief from conflict by bringing you down to their level. Little boys like to have someone in trouble with them, to share the blame and the shame. That is why some people want you to be like them. Do not be angry with their attempts to make you think their way. Do not respond to them in any way with impatience, even though they ridicule you. If you are better than they are, they may try to pull you down in order to feel that they are above you—if you oblige them, they will look down on you from their relative elevation. Desist from your efforts to make others feel better by cheering or comforting them. They need their discomfort if they are ever to find themselves.

Each time you meditate, you will gain a little more understanding, and your understanding will give you more strength to recognize and combat temptation.

Evil stress has a value for good. It provides the opportunity for virtue to appear. Each extension of love into a dark world strengthens and enlightens him who extends it, and simply seeing the evil becomes the evidence of good. As long as you are not angry and irritated at people or situations, you will have no compulsion to run, but will be able to face everything with wisdom and prudence.

Fear used to be the prime mover that gave you the energy to deal with problems. No more will this be true, for perfect love casts out fear. Your meditation exercise will allow the light of understanding to shine through you without interruption. It provides motivation to an inner pressure to be outspoken with firmness, kindness and patience. Don't try to learn these, or any other words by heart; merely let them lead you to the basic understanding, which is essentially a wordless communion with truth.

Do not be angry about the things people say. If words have made you angry in the past, let go of your reactions to them. You know that unrighteous anger creates fear. It is possible to develop fear of the effects of suggestion. We can waste our lives proving ourselves, proving others wrong, living on the defensive and offensive.

You must no longer be affected or impressed, except by what you know is right deep down inside. From now on, make allowances for the unkind words of others. Do not take personal offense. Right on the spot, be outspoken, without preparation, with firmness, kindness and patience. Truly, our whole life has been disturbed from its true course by our emotional reactions to what people have said about us, for or against us. Therefore, never be offended by anger or excited by praise. Neither must you be angry when you see that others are encouraging, "loving" and praising you only to weaken you.

The exercise brings about a response to truth as you see it in your inner perception of what is right each moment. It allows a decreasing response to conditions...and an increasing response to a divine plan from moment to moment... so that what you know is right for each moment will exact your loving obedience. Keep the basic understanding alive in your thoughts—not the exact words, but see and hear the meaning of them. Let your consciousness seek to be aware of what is wise and good.

Allow wisdom to extend into your daily life through the medium of meditation. Let this meditation and understanding become more joyful than the pleasure of things, so that your real happiness will come from doing what you know is fair and just.

Before the exercise came into your life, you reacted to conditions. The conditions affected your emotions, and your emotions controlled your thinking. Now, each time you meditate, your ability to alter your feeling and thinking to conform to a pattern of good will increase. This pattern of good, which appears as understanding, will drive your emotions, and your emotions will affect your reactions, and you will effortlessly affect for the better the conditions under which you live.

In other words, you will not react to injustice at home or at work. People will react to the justice in you and suffer the conflict that may bring them to repentance and salvation. Or, failing this, should they reject you and run away, you at least will be free. Your outspokenness will cause others either to respect you or to provide the persecution for righteousness' sake which, when met with love, is the spark of life eternal.

5

WHY WE ARE AFRAID

We have fear because we meet each moment unwisely, and unfairly. Animals cannot choose to be unfair or unwise; they are limited to one of two basic responses: run or fight. Technically, they are not afraid when they flee danger. They are simply stimulated in nature's way to outwit their adversary. They evolve stronger legs or wings or other mechanisms in this process. Their physical structure is maintained and developed by means of their reactions to the excitement of danger. If they run, they develop. If they become ferocious and fight back, they develop also. In either case, their reply to life's dangers is correct for them.

People, however, should not respond in the way of the animal inasmuch as they differ from the animal in one significant way; that is, they have reason. Reason or wisdom is a quality different from cunning or rationale. It is not a reaction to environmental stimulus. Cunning, on the other hand, is. It arises from a reaction of emotion, which bubbles into our minds as thought, which travels back through emotion into bodily activity.

Notice the cycle. It works like a computer. Fed the problem—two plus two, for instance—the computer replies with "four." So it is with growth. The danger represents the problem for our physical computer. It stimulates our emotions to produce a mental answer. The thought now patterns the bodily action. The sequence, repeated over a period of time, produces a habit pattern, and the answer becomes flesh. This is the evolutionary process, by means of which natural life is sustained. If you separated an animal from its environment, its body and mind would lose the sustaining factor and pattern of growth, and it would die. Yet man makes this very mistake when he tries to avoid feeling the fear, guilt and agony of not being able to meet each moment with wisdom and reason, for his natural environment is reason.

Each resentment is an attempt to reply to life and its challenges as an evolving beast. It causes us to feel, think and do terrible things. Once we are caught up in this animal cycle, any attempt to suppress our bubbling emotions makes us feel as though we were going to burst.

We may indeed distract ourselves from the disturbing parade of thoughts arising from our feelings, but that does not interrupt the process. We need larger amounts of pleasure, medication, drugs and distractions, all of which excite and disturb the body still more.

For man, any reaction based upon hostility bypasses the modifying factor of reason and prods his mind and body into mutilating changes that are proper for the beast but are guilt- and fear-producing in man.

Why does man react badly to irritants, temptation and

danger? It is because he does not love wisdom. He loves his own advantage. He has set his own goals and ambitions for life instead of seeking to discover what was prepared for him.

In order to have what he wants, he must deny the prod of reason toward what is prepared for him. Indeed, he must not even allow himself to see it for fear of being paralyzed into inaction by shame, disabled from pursuing the egocentric goals that the light of reality would show to be impossible of any real attainment. In the setting of his own path, man sets himself against the obedience to conscience and the world within. He seeks and needs support for his illusions and aspirations, for now he is minus the relationship with an inward stimulation from an inward world, out of which he could unfold to become different from the beast of the field. Man takes his shape and responses from what he stands next to.

Pursuing our own goals, we become sensitive to the forces of our outer environment. This consists of billions of other selfish men and women, also without reason, likewise maneuvering for their own advantage. They also spend their lives devising ways to stimulate, bamboozle and manipulate others to gain their own ends, blinding them to the light of reality that would disable their illicit schemes.

All is injustice; injustice because none of us will listen to the reason that haunts us as guilt whenever we fail to live rightly in any given moment. We live ambitiously, selfishly, blindly inflicting cruelties upon our fellows even as they inflict them upon us. We start by responding to another cunning manipulator who appeals to or supports our own ambitions (for his own good). We are excited by his wooing, and our consciousness is led captive into the powerful material world. It falls from reality into the realm of rationale and excuses. To escape from seeing our own weakness, we sit in judgment on our deceiver, and our own hostility toward him increases our sensitivity to life.

Hostility makes us feel right in our wrong, and our sense of rightness stimulates us to be aggressive. You see, we have lost the inner stimulation by virtue of our denial of it, by choosing our own ways, by allowing ourselves to be led into false beliefs. We have justified these ways as correct; we have rationalized them as right, and we have argued against our conscience, calling it wrong. All this is aided by more outside stimulus.

We have actually become enemies of reality! Because of this, we need the stimulation of the outer world to give us the drive that would otherwise come from within. But when the excitement comes along, it binds us even more closely to its controlling factor and separates us even more from what is right for that moment.

We need the stimulation of anger to feel right enough to move, but when we allow ourselves the luxury of hostility and impatience, our conscience pricks us and we become afraid of its light. We must flee to another excitement. And so it is that we grow to become dependent upon excitement. We need to be angry to live and move; but when we are, we find ourselves in bondage to an antagonistic world, guilty again, and because of this second guilt, more afraid. Everything we do when we are excited is wrong. We try to conceal our shame with excuses, but every excuse allows the ugly influences of the world to lead us to greater self-delusion, shame and fear.

Now we may try to find security from stress and tension in various comforts. We seek to escape our tensions in the pursuit of money, position and power. The challenge provides us with the stimulation we need to live, but in the end it kills us. For when we obtain the money, position and power, we find ourselves cut off from the very stimulation we have been living on. When we are moved by pressure, we die in metabolic confusion and fear—without pressure, we rot.

Meeting life with emotionalism, resentment and impatience, we are guilty of a deep wrong, and because of that guilt, we are afraid. Our first blind attempt at a solution is to find a life without temptation, pressure and trial. But in such a life, where we cannot exercise virtue and courage, we grow more guilty and afraid because of our failure to meet life at all.

So we grow afraid when we meet life, and also when we dodge life by protecting ourselves from those vital experiences that we must meet and cannot, for lack of reason. Once again, we must find that missing something and learn to live out of the inner stimulation that even now gently reminds us of our long-overlooked obligation to be human.

The foundation of courage is rightness. When we choose to deal fairly and deny personal ambition, advantage and gain in each moment of our contact with others, we are not subject to temptation, guilt and fear. Every wrong act that separates us from rightness carries with it guilt, and guilt always exudes the aura of fear (defensiveness or defiance).

We are guilty because we are wrong. We are wrong because we give up principles for personal ambition (ego). We can be made to fall only because our desire slopes toward the love of things before the love of the Maker of those things and that purpose for which both things and people were created.

Our need of people and things becomes necessary to nourish our sense of rightness—to support the proud and rebellious self that needs these possessions to uphold its glory. It is that desire to *be* the good—glorious, loved and worshiped—that subsequently sets us apart from the true Good.

No one can be tempted unless he desires what is offered,

so that when temptation comes our way we find ourselves giving up principle in favor of the fame, love and riches that we want. In this, our moment of truth, we move silently away from the secret essence of rightness that would hold us apart from any involvement with wrong, and the fear that wrong brings with it.

Observe the animals. Do they not have a certain strength that separates them from their enemy's belly? And when they fail in that strength, are not the barriers of life that hold these bodies apart torn down? Does not the unfitness of the one to live result in his becoming food for the victor?

It is much the same with us. The love of rightness keeps us this side of temptation, so that we grow in strength in the face of each tempter. The temptation serves as a call to that strength and tests the loyalty of the soul.

When we desire advantage, gain, admiration and approval, we have (by that selfish desire) betrayed a preordained purpose, and in so doing we set ourselves against reality. So when our temptation (stimulus) comes, we speak and act "lovingly," but only for the purpose of bringing our ambition to fruition. Always we are living falsely and pretentiously, lying. We are never truly kind. The very idea of kindness becomes perverted in us and leads to more error and fear.

Perhaps, in falling, we feel empty, guilty, afraid, angry, disgusted or furious at those people and things which promised to make us right and powerful. But it is the acceptance of those things that promised so much support to our pride that made us wrong, not so much the temptation itself.

Now we need more of those things to make us feel right again, so we find ourselves subject to more temptation, which leads to more error and guilt in place of the glory and advantage we desired. And so we become a slaves of that which promises us what it cannot give (which is something it really wants from us instead).

Why are we slaves? Because as long as we continue in our ambition, we shall always need the substance of that continuance. The things we "need" are needed to remedy our fears and guilts.

But in reality, we are denying the true remedy and correction. The guilt and fear we feel is a warning flag, designed to lure us back from our journey into hell. Being proud, and still wanting to chart our own course (which we do not realize is a compass setting to Hades), we try to bypass the correction with various methods. We renew our efforts to obtain love and money to drown out that sense of guilt, but we are left with even more of the same, so we make our usual proud attempts to eradicate the problem of our guilty conscience. We have embarked on a strange voyage. We maneuver for the pleasures of life to support our ambition, but soon after the effect of feeling better has passed, we feel worse than ever, for we have become more wrong in the process, serving evil as we would have it serve us.

To be brave it is necessary to oppose and overcome. But when we need people, we dare not oppose them. We must cater to them to obtain our objectives and uphold our illusions, and to do this, we must live untruthfully. It is this untruthfulness that makes us afraid. When we have lost what it takes to overcome fear, we must also give in to others to avoid the stress that makes us afraid, but then we are serving the sin in others and not living rightly, so we continue to grow more afraid.

Not knowing where we are going is another fear producer. Anyone who has walked in total darkness where there has been no light to show the way knows the fear that arises from not knowing where the next step will take him. So it is with us. When we move away from the progression of rightness, we move in the dark. We cannot make decisions—or if we do, and they turn out well, we are pained by the success. In other words, what we receive pains us as much as what is withheld. We may wind up doing nothing for fear of being a success or a failure, hoping thereby to conquer our fear, but then we cease to live—and that is enough to make anybody afraid.

We are afraid because we are wrong. We are wrong because our personal ambition stands in the way of what is right each moment. If we had no vanity to satisfy, we could be tempted by nothing. We could not respond. Therefore, we could not become involved in the process that leads to guilt and fear.

In order to possess courage, we must patiently bear painful pressures and conquer our tendency to conform. The happiness and security gained from this ability far exceeds the false comfort and safety we would have retained by yielding to pressure.

Fear increases as we fall away from principle. Nothing can relieve the misery created by this fall. Only a person who lives from the inner intuitive impulse of right, ignoring consequence, will conquer all fear.

Man's invisible enemy is unnatural fear; i.e., fear that is set in motion by emotional upset and frustration, fear which cannot be conquered simply by facing the condition, as is the case in our ordinary apprehensions. Normal apprehension is merely sensible caution, and can be alleviated through the application of reason; but the frustration of being unable to fulfill our ambition is the greatest single source of fear in man today.

As long as we are wrong in our relationship to life, we

need emotional feelings to feel alive and right. When we need to be upset to feel right, and excited to feel loved, we not only grow more wrong, but we increase our need for the very emotion we should be conquering. In order to mature, we must conquer our emotional reactions.

So fear arises because 1) we are wrong in using emotion to rise above situations and to make us feel right when we are not right and 2) therefore, we cannot conquer the emotionality because we *need* it. Under the circumstances, we cannot be courageous at all, because we need the stimulation provided by the people we should be opposing.

When animals are threatened, their natural reaction is to run or fight. But when we desert wisdom and strike out in anger, we are wrong. If we are fearful, or if we become frustrated and annoyed and suppress these reactions, we are running away, which is also wrong. Everything we say and do in anger and with ambition is wrong. It leads to guilt—and to fear because of that guilt. Even if you save a little boy from drowning—if you act out of fear or pressure, your motivation is wrong. On the other hand, everything we say and do without anger or without selfish ambition is right.

Fear is a direct result of a compulsive reflex reaction to conditions. Hostility bypasses reason and evinces our lack of inner relatedness. Reaction always produces unwholesome thought cycles, which bubble up from below, rather than from the above (within). Such thoughts, projected back through the emotions, emerge in destructive ways and cause us to grow as animals do. This process is similar to that which takes place in the sleeping person who feels as though he is falling because of what he is dreaming. Another example: when we vengefully plan to hurt another, we often experience the feeling that this other person is presently persecuting us.

When the proud "self-atoning" person endeavors to discover why he feels guilty or afraid, he must necessarily find the wrong reasons because he won't admit the truth. When his problem-solving self-analysis fails to work, he is again upset and frustrated. This frustration turns to negative thought, which in turn can become worry, which in turn causes more problems and fears arising from the frustration at being unable to resolve the previous difficulty.

The whole cycle is fed and kept alive by continued failure to respond rightly to conditions. This rut is called compulsion. It can become quite involved, enslaving us to ineffectual remedies, which we hope will change conditions but which only cause us to be afraid to take a new lease on our lives. More important, all compulsion is simply evidence of a deep-seated spiritual wrong, which we will rarely admit. It may be too frightening to consider at this time, but it will become apparent as you progress. You will come to see that the fear of the Lord is the beginning of wisdom.

Emotion-produced thought is similar to a compulsive meditation. The repetitious dwelling upon an idea produces a devolutionary progression to other problems. Physical symptoms soon manifest the effect of this growing error. Suppose we take fear and guilt and dwell upon them, trying to understand and solve them. In the process we develop more complicated symptoms. Compulsive "meditation" upon a problem is called worry, an activity that has been set into motion by frustration (being upset or angry). The problem-solving activity of the foolish ego is called worry. Blind worry adds impetus to the problem and often draws to us the very thing we fear. Nagging thoughts caused by our upsets can cause us to do the very thing we dread or detest, just to get it off our minds. But it does not succeed. We are only

100

upset again when we discover that we have compounded our problem by taking the wrong action, and added, in the vain hope of relieving the feeling, more compulsive worry as a result of being upset over our newer blunders.

Thus, we are caused to think about resolving the newer problems. The pride that allowed the problem to grow up in us in the first place is the same blind pride that constantly creates more problems through being challenged to solve them. When we are upset, we repeat the same cycle of activity that originally created the fears. We could not be upset or frustrated if we had no vanity or concupiscent goals.

The prod of environment stimulates the animal to grow and evolve. The animal takes its nature from the programming call of life. However, when we experience this response in ourselves, we usually do not dare to allow such a nature to express itself openly. This animal-like call to "growth" is the evidence of our wrong, our spiritual incompleteness, and its expression or suppression reveals our fear.

Sometimes we can identify the object of our fear by looking at our resentments, for what we resent the most, we fear the most. If we cannot throw off our resentments, we will do terrible things. Or we are compelled to resort to strange, useless remedies and rituals for relief, but the relief only creates more tension.

To escape from our fear, we may experience the desire to "get away from it all"; to keep moving from one town to another; to travel or to wander from one job to another, from one wife to another. Or we may try to escape to situations that promise relief, apparent safety and peace. Some people are always "iffing" like this—running to the opposite condition to find calmness and freedom from the discomfort that arises from their unrelatedness to a higher self. However, in our "repose," the excitement that we need to remedy our conscience is not present, so we become more afraid than ever. Furthermore, we become more fearful because we are not exercising virtue and facing up to life's problems.

Usually, because of unresolved resentments and guilts, we pick inferior, less principled persons for our new associates. Around them we appear less guilty, even superior and unafraid. But soon we are upset again into more resentment and panic through some petty injustice. We can't live with these new friends because we are upset, but we can't live without them because we need the excitement provided by the contrast of their greater wrongness to minimize our own growing guilts and fears.

Strangely, we need to be upset to feel right, and to maintain our pride we must continue to be upset, but to be upset is wrong—and so is the pride that it feeds. To overcome our fears, of course, we need to conquer our emotions under stress. Only when we become stronger than what threatens us are we no longer threatened and no longer afraid. But pride needs emotional support through praise or resentment to feel alive and right. Because we want to fulfill pride's unholy need, we will not and cannot overcome the emotions that are overcoming us and making us more wrong and afraid. We shall eventually discover that we are being controlled by those who allow us the luxury of being upset, since we are becoming more responsive to them and their secret demands, which they enforce by triggering our guilt feelings. Perhaps we shall then overcome our secret emotions with a burst of temper to frighten them away, but that makes us more of a beast, less human in our behavior, with more reason to be afraid.

In close places, or in crowds, panic can develop because

movement is limited and there is no way of escape when our reaction to the presence of so many people increases our uneasiness. Animals that are cornered will panic. Timid creatures who normally run may become vicious under these conditions, as the feeling-to-run changes into the feeling-to-fight. Escape from the intolerable may come to us in the form of unconsciousness (fainting), or escape into sickness to win sympathy and thus avoid the attacks that we cannot bear. After a while, the very presence of people can cause discomfort, irritation and even panic.

When we are upset, we may express it through one of two completely opposite (on the surface, at least) natures: one is overly nice and passive; the other is rude and aggressive. The overly-kind personality uses sweetness as a weapon, to keep conditions good so as to avoid being upset (afraid). The aggressive personality also strives to avoid becoming upset, but his method is to get in the first punch and upset the other fellow. Both of them are trying to prevent their own reactions by getting others to react, becoming a threat in order to escape the pressure that will reveal them as they are: proud, frightened, unrepentant, inadequate. Extremely opposite personalities emerge, depending on the individual's abilities and propensities, but the intent is the same in either case.

When extremists (as described above) become parents, they project the same confusion to their offspring, who conform to or rebel against the pressures of extremism. They too are tempted away from right, and their selfhood is violated. Afraid and too proud to admit error, they utilize the powers of rebellion to frighten others. Or they may try to "sweeten" others into not opposing them, thereby becoming just like their conformist parents.

We all find a sense of rightness in comparing ourselves

with others—which is wrong—which is again fear. Wherever you find fear, you will find anger. For example, if I push someone who cannot swim into the water, even though I bring him out quickly, he may become angry because I frightened him.

An alcoholic may strike someone while under the influence of drink, then become afraid to drink again, and resent the other person for this restriction of his pleasure. Through the tension created out of resentment, the desire to drink grows so great that the repression reaches unbearable proportions and produces more fear—fear that he might drink and misbehave again.

The very "honesty" that so many of us lay claim to originated in our fear of the consequences of dishonesty. We may resent the pressure that we need to control us, and the more we resent it, the more we bend over backwards to hide our resentment with a great show of adherence and conformity. But as long as we persist in our secret anarchistic desires and animal reaction, our responses for or against the various pressures that keep us in line will increase, and so will our fear.

Virtuous courage is the ability to face discomfort, persecution and trial without resentment. Hostility decreases the inherent ability to withstand pressure and pain. Hostility causes us to fall from a calm impersonal viewpoint and gives rise to the need for pleasure which, being wrong, causes guilt and fear.

By striving to live a pain-free life, we fill our lives with pain. We try to escape pain in pleasure, only to find that pleasure is not an antidote for pain, so our pain increases. The fact is that we should never have had the pain that calls for pleasure—we should never have been moved from an original state of calmness.

No matter where we point the finger, the thing that caused our fall was our resentment. Resentment is an increasing, uncontrolled response to the negative, to what is unpleasant.

It causes us to withdraw from the unpleasant condition and seek out pleasure to soothe the psychic pain. But the less we deal with small painful experiences in the present, the less we are able to do so in the future. By failing to meet the painful experience correctly, we grow more fearful and more sensitive to pain because we have chosen to escape it. We try to avoid feeling afraid by not facing what makes us afraid, but our failure to exercise courage leads us to a greater fear. Moreover, we tend to win the approval of what should be opposing us to bring forth that courage.

We often think, "I would be all right if they would be all right." So we set out to placate the resented ones, trading off self-respect and principle, inch by inch, day by day, for peace at any price. However, people now see this as a lack of self-respect and are inspired to take advantage—they start to create more of the painful upsets we have schemed to avoid, and because they resent our attempts to mold their lives, they rebel and purposely try to hurt, frustrate, or scare us away from being "nice."

The externally-motivated mind is subject to the mood of the body—and to the world. It can never be healed. Why? First, because by laboring for peace (from an externally-motivated frame of reference), we give up the very value that could make us peaceful and well. Second, the perfect outside condition, if ever attained, becomes the matrix of more fear and disease. Why? Because we grow fearless, peaceful and noble only in the face of that which threatens to deprive us of these qualities.

Love and courage are feelingless states of being. When we burn a finger, it feels bad, but when we counteract the pain with a soothing balm, it feels good. Truly, it is not better. That feeling is an illusion arising out of the contrast of relief. Our own false remedy substitutes for the real balm of healing. So when, through not being wise, we fall and "burn our finger," instead of seeking that original painless state, we seek the soothing "balm" for relief, the pleasure substitute for true health and happiness. Unfortunately, we find ourselves needing pain as our pleasurable feeling wears off. What we should prefer is that original feelingless (but not insensitive) state of being.

Unfortunately, we tend to run to greater extremes to soothe the pain of falling from our original state. We set about so busily and so desperately to repair the damage—as though it were noble to do so, and as though we deserve the relief we seek. In doing so, we beget more pain because we become more wrong in substituting pleasure for the joy which we could experience if we were not feeling-based. One day we may not be able to purchase or obtain enough relief or good feelings for our growing agony, and we shall be left without the wherewithal to do so in an eternal fire of guilt.

Upon reacting with hostility, we feel pain or fear— perhaps even the guilt that gives rise to pain and fear. Struggling to overcome our uncomfortable reactions, we douse ourselves with medication or seek to distract ourselves with pleasure. We fight or we run. But nothing avails, as we have fallen from our calm, neutral position of observation. All those who fear are separated from the reality within by their emotional responses and their proud remedies.

Often we try to offset our fear and pain by moving toward what appears to be the opposing value in the world, bravado and pleasure—but these are not the true opposites. The very motion toward a self-chosen remedy produces a greater motion away from the solution within. Thus we have more pain at the end of pleasure, more resentment against that pain, and fear because of the resentment.

Seeking happiness, foolish people must unconsciously draw pain to themselves so that they may know and enjoy pleasure. Eventually they can no longer find enough pleasure to ease the pain, so they are left with the pain. To most pleasure-seeking people death represents the end of pleasure and sensation. The more we seek pleasure, the more we beget pain, which must be soothed by more pleasure. The need for protection, pleasure and ease grows to frightening proportions.

Pleasure produces a counterfeit happiness that can exist only as long as pleasure is pleasant. We often fear death because we have built our values around sensation, and death would expose us to an eternal, burning hunger that cannot be satisfied without a body to serve as a vehicle for sensation. On the other hand, we may look forward to death as a release from the torture of not finding satisfaction in pleasure.

Whenever we find fear, we find one of two extreme attitudes: a mad, frustrating pursuit of pleasure, or a state of withdrawal from life and its power to hurt. As long as we succeed in allaying our fears with laughter and pleasure, we spurn the value of virtue, but the less virtuous we are, the more afraid we become. The temporary success of our remedies allows us to travel farther away from rightness, but finally, a time comes when all remedies fail us, and then we feel the accumulation of our error as fear, sickness and despair.

There must come a moment in our lives when we need the courage we did not develop—when we look in a full-length mirror and see there not a person, but a mountain of nervous jelly filled with tranquilizers.

There is no substitute on earth for courage. However, the conquest of fear requires the conquest of daily frustration. To accomplish this end, we must find within our innermost being a desire to place principles before our personal aims and advantage. We must be willing to live and speak up for the things we know to be right in our hearts. We must hold fast to our true convictions and exercise them even though we might be hurt by our stand in virtue. We must seek redemption from our fall from reality. Although we have no desire to hurt, we must realize that truth does bring pain, both to ourselves and to those we love, but that pain is a stress that we need if we are to grow.

Above all, we must not be tempted to resent or respond to those who try to torment us away from our clear perception of their weaknesses. If we want to avoid hurting the feelings of others, it is because the image we have of ourselves will be disturbed when their reaction upsets us. Consequently, we are really attempting to serve our own interests when we fail to speak up for what is right. We are guilty within ourselves for our failure to act rightly.

Suppose for a moment that we desire to speak and act rightly, but our first words cause a negative reaction in the person we are talking to, and we react to his reaction with hostility. Our reaction washes away reasonable disagreement and makes us disagreeable instead. The good words and deeds that we originally had in mind are transformed by our emotions into unkind words and actions. We may be horrified at the substitution of bad for good and fail to express anything. We can become choked up and unable to speak because our realization tells us we are unwise. This is the case with millions who stutter, procrastinate and otherwise find expression difficult under emotional stress.

On the other hand, many respond to motivation and pressure with false courage, and this also leads to trouble. They become involved with intrigue, champion false causes, and in their need for substitute courage and rightness, are easily led by others.

No matter what causes resentment, it is an emotion with a consistent quality. How we express it will depend on our education and background, but the emotion itself remains the same. Resentment leads to resentment, and we make excuses and bigger blunders, leading to more resentment and blame, guilt, and the fear that guilt brings with it. Resentment is the emotion that supports the ego's judgment. It is the stimulus that makes us all feel right—but that peculiar illusion is in reality another layer of wrong. So we need to be upset to feel right again.

The ego, being wrong in its struggle to appear right, grows more afraid. Hostility is always the unmistakable evidence of a wrong trying to be a right, but becoming more guilty and afraid in the process.

It is remarkable how irritating small frustrations can be. You are ready to go to church when a friend telephones. He is in a talkative mood. But you happen to be late. Everyone is waiting, but your friend continues talking, unaware of your need to hurry. You think to yourself, "I wish he would shut up and let me get out of here," but you say nothing. Rather than hurt his feelings, you become torn between the need to be gone and the phone conversation.

Now if you were inspired by true principle, you could say to your friend, "Excuse me, Joe; the family is waiting outside in the car—we were just leaving when you called. I will call you tonight when I have more time." This would release you in a natural manner from the obligation to listen—it would be an honest expression of your situation. Instead, you seize upon the opportunity to judge the presumptuousness of your friend; you become more angry with him each moment. You blame him for his intrusion, and in so doing, divert your attention from your own weakness. You feel guilty for failing to meet the moment with the virtue of patience, and out of this guilt comes fear. Out of fear comes the desire to please, expressed in the idea of not wanting to hurt someone's feelings. In this way you condition yourself to be inconvenienced the same way in the future to make up for your past guilts!

So we end up by being "kind," but in a manner that is destructive to us and to our friend.

A child may resent the over-discipline and criticism of his father. The emotion causes his thoughts to grow more and more hostile as they dwell on the resentment that he dares not express. His little mind grows so filled with hate that he has to be very careful what he says, lest he speak his mind and get into trouble. Having been upset away from his inner common sense, he is at a loss for words. He begins to look for something to say other than what is on his mind. He blurts out the first safe thing that comes to his mind, but it doesn't make sense, so he draws more criticism, to which he reacts with greater resentment, and the cycle starts over again.

Worry over the situation only makes it worse, and an outsider's attempt to ease the tension by being polite only releases a greater flood of anger and reactivates the cycle.

Every stutterer will tell you that he worries about what he is going to say. He is not so much worried as careful. He is afraid of saying the wrong things, because this draws criticism, which also makes him angry and afraid. He is paralyzed also because he is preoccupied with searching for a good place to begin.

The catalyst of good speech is a single-minded attentiveness to common sense for that moment. From this springs a steady flow of related facts and insights. When we are upset we lose our focus, and our speech no longer flows gracefully from its source toward its objective. Our reaction causes ugly thoughts to arise in our minds from another source, thoughts that we dare not express. We lose sight of reason and, searching for a word or sentence to get us back on the track, we become more afraid to speak for fear of making another mistake.

Many stammerers speak fluently when they become angry because anger creates a "don't care" feeling. As long as their anger is expressed, the ugliness just "flows over the dam." Sometimes people afflicted with speech difficulties need just the opposite condition: a complete absence of stress. I remember an announcer who could speak fluently before a microphone, but he stammered badly in face-to-face encounters.

Angry people often seem to be industrious individuals as they work off their surplus emotion on people or projects. A hostile person is not an industrious or brave person, however. All of us can accomplish much under the compulsion of fear or anger, but that accomplishment is unrewarding since the activity takes us farther away from our calm center. Its only intention is to make us look and feel right inside, but it never quite succeeds, no matter how dazzling our performance might appear to the on-looker.

Fear of heights is symbolic of the instability of pride. Resentment causes us to slip our moorings and grow more helpless in the face of stress, stress being any situation that places us in any kind of danger. Our guilts, worries and fears cause us to become sickly and accident-prone—and we hold up our weaknesses as a shield to protect us from further stress, or we use them to play on the guilts and weaknesses of others in order to get their sympathy or financial assistance.

In order to escape from observing our weakness, we may

blame a situation or a parent, usually a parent, for our failures. This blame, because it "justifies" our wrong, keeps us in error and causes us to become more afraid. It keeps us in bondage to the response patterns that cause fear and suffering. As hostility grows within us, it may cause us to become afraid of hurting others in our anger. Big, strong individuals often become overly timid with people because they fear their own strength and dread what they might do in a moment of anger. Unfortunately, their timidity is seen as weakness and people take advantage of it anyway—sometimes enough to upset such individuals into doing the very things they fear.

You see, they don't want to hurt others—but only in pride's way. Their love for others is not really love at all; if it were, they could not be upset. They need to be upset to feel right— then they seize upon their restraint and see it as kindness.

Summing up: with each successive annoyance, we grow weaker and more sensitive to our environment, until the most trivial condition will appear to be an unbearable pressure on us. We come to resent the work we are chained to, that we actually need, if only in order to obtain funds to soothe our agonies, or to appease demanding people, or to pay (hated) doctor bills, or to buy new cars and status symbols to cover up our inferiority feelings.

All the material things we buy to support the happiness of our pride makes us more miserable and resentful. We resent the things, as well as the people, that give us pain and fear instead of the healing balm they seemed to promise.

Resentment is constantly building upon itself, causing the body to react in various negative ways. When we face a situation containing the elements of danger, we become unable to meet it with wisdom because of our previous conditioning. Resentment has led us to knowledge of fear, the desire to run and to take action contrary to reason. Our un-wise responses have created bigger problems for us to become upset over. The experience now adds worry to refuel the fire. Only a patient, calm, positive man can successfully handle a negative situation.

Resentment causes us to become controlled increasingly by circumstances as opposed to the framework of reason—we lose the natural spontaneity that would enable us to handle difficult situations gracefully, with a light touch.

The angry man is ill-equipped to face life. He has no dominion over things. On the contrary, things gain dominion over him. He overrides cruelty with greater cruelty and folly with greater folly. In the process, he develops frustration, anger and fear. His resentment causes him to become unable to express himself reasonably; he becomes choked up and emotionally blocked.

A man who responds is the emotional servant of those who cause him to respond. A man who does not bear witness to the truth in word and deed, and is unable to change things around him, becomes a doormat for others. He becomes more and more submissive, compromising to avoid being hurt.

When things are good he feels good, so at the first sign of danger he tries to buy peace. He does this especially with his enemies because it is they who are most likely to deprive him of his peace. He cannot stand any disturbance because he is already disturbed by his chaotic emotions. Conditions must be good for him to feel good, and to this end he strives with great cunning.

When things are not good, and he cannot make them so, he panics. He becomes a slave of those who know his needs and who pretend to fulfill them...he then gives his tormentors what they want.

Is that peace? No. It is more guilt and, because of guilt, fear. He is at peace with his enemy but at war with himself.

Resentment is the service of hell in man, and disobedience to God. The average man is found in the full-time occupation of serving or appeasing his enemies and taking out his frustrations on those he claims to love.

The angry man can think "good" only when conditions are good. His error causes him to fear people and to need their approval. But when we seek approval from other people in order to remain calm and unafraid, we become artificial—like the actor on the stage—a hollow shell under the outward niceties.

The over-ambitious salesman soon finds it difficult to work. Those he "sells" are weaklings (already oversold by other ambitious salesmen), and he resents their dishonesty when they fail to pay their bills. Soon he is afraid of selling because it is wrong to motivate, because of the frustrations and disappointments and because of his own rage. Each succeeding wrong response to life has added to his guilt and the "feeling-to-run." Soon the fear of hurting his pride may make it impossible for him to go to work at all. Or he may decide to make selling secondary, and bend his major effort toward making people like him. But if he succeeds in this, he cannot sell, because he now likes the client too much and is embarrassed to "sell" a friend; so he gives his merchandise away. At the same time, he becomes afraid to hear a "no" that will shatter the sensitive pride that he has built up by manipulating "yeses." Then too he is upset by criticism from his wife or family for giving everything away or not selling it all.

The woman who was frightened by a mouse will not say to the next mouse she encounters, "I'm not scared of you, because you're not the mouse that scared me in the first place."

One hundred mice will have one hundred times the effect of one mouse. And so it is with the fear of people and crowds.

Accumulating resentment can cause that disorganized expression known as epilepsy, as well as an increased sensitivity to the smallest irritations that manifests as allergy. Problems rarely stem from one incident of anger, but rather from a continuous, accumulating reaction pattern that grows each day, unless we recognized it and change from now on.

Anger represents our inability to forgive, and our inability to forgive is our insensibility to the principle of love.

Fear is the motivation of the beast, the evidence of man's failure to find the impetus of love.

"He who hath fear is not made perfect in love."

6

MEDITATION AS THE WAY TO COURAGE

Each time you overlook on the spot and are outspoken—with firmness, kindness, and patience—you are developing (among other things) courage. As long as you are patient, you will be free from beastly extremes of behavior; your patience will increase your ability to stand unmoved in the face of trials. Everything you say or do will flow effortlessly from what you perceive in calmness.

It used to be that you were upset and said the wrong thing—or you were upset and said nothing. Now, the process within you is reversing itself; you are not upset, and you say or do something reasonable—or you are not upset, and you say or do nothing, in accordance with reasonable requirements of the moment.

Do not blame others, nor look into the past for the original cause of your trouble. You already know what it is. It is pride supported by the emotion of hostility. It continues to feed and multiply your problems, upset by upset.

From now on, just watch and observe calmly. As you recognize your anger patterns, merely observe your related weaknesses and resentments and allow them to pain you. Refrain from correcting your own faults. The stress of realizing our inability to make ourselves right will become repentance, and repentance stresses the compassion of the Father to grace us with the remedy.

Be patient with what you see within, as well as without. When you do not allow the injustice of others to puff up your pride with judgment or challenge you to deal with the threat to your ego, the spirit within you is stressed to reply for you. Soon you will be able to see and overcome hostilities you have not even noticed as yet (because of their subtlety), just by watching and not being upset by what you see. Each time you succeed, true courage will emerge and fear will fall away.

In the past, you were afraid to observe life as it was, perhaps because of the violence of your reactions to what you observed. You could not deal wisely with what you saw, so you chose to see less and less. Now you must observe the cruelties of life, and yet stand unmoved by them—allow a nature deep within to deal with each threat. You may feel as though your experiences were not actually happening to you, as though someone other than yourself were experiencing life for you.

In much the same manner, when we play god to our children, we react for them in time of danger, robbing them of that experience within—making them dependent upon us, as they would otherwise be on God. You will see problems that your ego was never able to cope with being resolved effortlessly by the self you had once lost touch through your reaction to your parents.

The process of self-alienation began with your first obvious error: becoming upset and judging the cruelties of others. The second mistake was trying to compensate for the problems and fears that arose in you as a consequence of that personal reply of hostility. This, of course, only compounded the problem. A consciousness that allowed that response to begin with is in dereliction. Being in error, it cannot correct itself.

The meditation exercise restores your relatedness to truth and reason via repentance. It allows for a spiritual refueling in that extra moment you act. Patiently waiting for the intuitive prod to right thought or action, you will no longer be thinking in terms of your own advantage, or fearing consequences.

Fear of pain (consequences) brings only greater pain. Whatever method you had by which you used to control uneasiness (guilt) will soon fall away. You will become insured by hope as you move from one perception of reality to another. Fear of decisions arose because your insight was distorted by emotions, feelings, responses and hungers, all of which led you to make more mistakes. There is always an element of fear when we cannot see rightly, when we walk in the darkness of our own ambitions and the excuses for them that once passed for reason.

You should learn to trust your perception of outside reality—you should always have listened to what you knew was right within yourself. As you become more patient, the mist of emotion and fear will no longer cloud your reason, so that truth for each moment will be plain to see and it will be easy to function from what is wise and good. Since you always perceive what is right and true for each moment, you will never need to make decisions through analysis.

Life is like a voyage through time. You have been given so many years in which to gather the treasures of love, courage and wisdom. In the matrix of patience, everything grows as a matter of course, without struggle. So do not be in a hurry for any results. Keep your entire being fixed upon the good principles you are discovering with joy, and rewards will appear on their own in ways you least expect. Just keep your mind on basic principles. They will become the cause of better effects to come.

If you worry about developing or ridding yourself of symptoms, you will not be able to keep your attention upon the principle that will bring about the real solution. It is the principle that leads to the hope of a cure, not your will aided by the force of impatience, or by any outward assurance. Love of truth leads to the courage of one's own convictions, and courage grows to dispel the mists of fear and despair.

Through the meditation exercise, you will discover the meaning of love, and then you will find that courage, happiness and health will follow naturally, without strain or effort. Your doubts and fears will suddenly seem pointless, and they will dissolve from your mind as you recognize this fact. They were nothing but an evolution of guilts which originated through illicit ambitions and being upset—they had no other basis for being. Now that you are becoming more and more patient and relaxed, the old fears, excuses and guilts are starved of their power to grow (by your right response), and must therefore fall away.

Your mind is becoming free from its preoccupation with seeking solutions that only create bigger problems. You will lose interest in many things that you erroneously believed to be important, and soon you will have time to ponder and wonder and see life as it really is, instead of just worrying about it. You will never feel compelled to do this meditation exercise. It will never become a habit. It must be what you choose to do voluntarily each morning. By willingly doing the exercise each morning, you will effortlessly be able to follow the principle of patience and tolerance, which you are discovering and which is being set in motion from within through your sincere desire. By doing so, you free your mind and body from old, useless, mechanical ideas and from worry, fear and habit. By choosing to do the exercise and binding yourself through free will to this new source of information, you unchain yourself from externalized, compulsive behavior and the monotonous pursuit of pleasure and comfort.

Now that you are being set free from your fear, make sure you are not tripped up by getting angry over natural feelings you experience. Meeting a new situation is very often accompanied by natural sensations of weakness and anticipation, sometimes felt in the pit of the stomach. Understand that this is natural, and do not get angry with yourself for experiencing it. That would create more fear. Natural apprehension is a necessary call to virtue, which emerges when you desist from getting excited. Your only real enemy is your pride, and its use of anger and fear to deal with temptation and danger. You must overcome the temptation to deal with problems with your own faculties of mind and emotion. Quiet the egotistical response, and allow wisdom and love to move through you in each moment of stress.

Be sure that you do not blame any person, or continue to look for any condition in your life to blame for your present difficulties. Continued resentments are subconsciously designed to relieve you of responsibility by fixing the entire blame for your inferiorities and weaknesses on other people. This only produces more fear and enslavement to error. If your fault is entirely another's, then it follows that you are not wrong—and if you are right, why would you want to change?

It is easy to blame certain conditions for our failures in life, but our blame constitutes escape from guilt, adds more hostility, and prevents us from going forward as we should. Adversities do not cause our troubles. They only bring our weakness to light.

What is frightening to one person is strengthening to another. A person who learns to be tolerant in life's small issues can face greater problems to come. Irritability, impatience, hostility, regardless of what causes them, rob us of the ability to be virtuously brave.

There are three ways to face threat: fight, run, or remain calm. Sometimes it is correct to be righteously indignant,to speak with conviction. As long as you do not have the desire to hurt, retaliate, or prevail animalistically and egotistically, you will be able speak and act with a clear mind. This kind of strength enables you to see and challenge the wrong of others without rudeness, and you will succeed in making wrongdoers ashamed of themselves. Then the error in others will retreat, and the truth within you will advance.

All fear stems from our unmodified reaction to stress. It began when we first allowed our consciousness to be tempted down by praise or criticism. To be moved by fear is to be guilty of meeting a moment incorrectly. Fear can be conquered only by learning to come back to the conscious state that existed before our first experience of fear.

Man should deal with problems of stress in a way that is different from that of animals. In him, reason must intercede to cancel the compulsion to develop in the flesh. That is to say, the growth in flesh is an inhuman complex of development for man. It is a compensation. This kind of growth promotes fear in us.

Wrong inner relatedness manifests itself outwardly as

a physical neurosis of some sort, a lopsided clumsiness in dealing with problems; i.e., a jerky gait, perhaps, or an all-thumbs awkwardness when working with the hands. Every compensation demands a physical development. There are terrifying situations, however, where no physical compensation can take place. It would be difficult to become bigger and stronger than a thunderstorm or a petty remark.

For man, any fleshly answer evokes the complex evolutionary laws, and it is a fall away from reason's refinement. If man were meant to be an evolving animal, his emotional response to pressure would be a healthy one. But it most certainly is not. Emotional response, for man, is productive of nothing but fear, guilt, disease and death. Eventually we may learn to fear our emotions.

When we respond, we feel emotion, and when our response is to the outside world, it conflicts with our intuitive knowledge of what is timely for us (conscience). This conflict produces guilt—hence, fear. Emotion triggers a system of development that runs counter to our real human nature. The temptation is to blame the source of stress for our plight, and to destroy or appease it; but it is not entirely responsible—we share the responsibility by reason of our response to it.

Emotional responsiveness evinces our individual failure to find virtue's essence, the humanizing essence of patience, often called love. Our emotional dilemma is the witness of a deep-seated disparity. It continues to be that witness as it compels us toward the development of beastly cravings and unearthly desires, which weigh heavily on our conscience. This development continues its disturbing progress until we search for the "ectoplasm" of truth and learn how to resolve emotion.

We must have emotion, of course, but reason must be

the trigger. Intuition, not instinct, must be the source of information to our feelings. Before a person can be afraid, he must be led down from reason. This can be accomplished only by a response to temptation.

What has not found love tempts by default. Generally speaking, it was our parents who failed us. Careful! Although our parents should have touched us with human understanding, we must remember that they, too, were children of unreasonable parents, as were their parents before them. Our continued resentment (blame) toward what they passed on to us through blindness of heart is the cause of our continued failing in all things, just as their resentment (self-justification) toward their parents put the seal on what they themselves became.

Hate is not a reasonable defense against hatred. Hating back continues our separation from reason and causes us to develop in the way of animals. It also assures our likeness to those we hate. You have grounds to resent your parents, granted. But you must realize that your continued hostility, although justified, is not just, and it binds you to the process that produces fear. Only the response of love (patience) can truly separate us from what is wrong.

We have a right to be wrong, but that does not make our wrong right. In our secret hostility, the sense of right we feel is egocentric. Indulging in it, we are the judge and the jury, and occasionally, the executioner.

Resentment is the ectoplasm of self-righteousness and the substance of the error of fear. As long as we believe ourselves to be already correct, we cannot receive what will make us right. Only when we realize the wickedness of anger can we discover in ourselves what will make us truly right. However, before we can receive the correction, we must admit our mistake and be sorry.

Sin is transmitted through the judgement the elevated, prideful ego enjoys when it sees that others are wrong. Our self-righteous ego delights in the wrongness of others (who, incidentally, are also intoxicated with their own false righteousness). Our observation of their faults provides us with the temptation to judge (which makes us become like them), and to feel power and glory. Responding to the call of pride, we are denied the fulfillment of God within. But if we are willing to be shown, responding to temptation eventually reveals to us the flaw in the nature that we have inherited. We must learn to resolve this through repentance (being sorry).

All of us learn, usually at an early age, to gorge ourselves on everything that gratifies our ego. Soon we are disqualified as humans. We forget love, justice and mercy for each moment. In the twinkling of an eye we lose altitude and forget who and what we are. Then, for a long time, we see very little, except troubles and woes, guilts and fears that grow and grow.

We finally exhaust our only two possible alternatives for dealing with problems and dangers. We try being nice, then we try getting mad, but neither works. We try to conquer what was conquering us, and we only become a bigger animal, and more afraid because of what we did in order to overcome. We try to give up or hide, only to grow more afraid because of our failure to meet life at all. We cannot really succeed in our attempts to become a bigger bully or a bigger hero. Even as heroes we shall feel afraid, because what we have done to be brave is simply to win the admiration of fools, needing (yet maybe hating) their applause as evidence of our courage. If we manage to accept their homage as truth, we become dependent upon their applause for our illusion of virtue and courage, and separate ourselves further and further from reason.

All fear intensifies as it drives us to compensate for our lack of patience. That is, it tempts us to wrestle with problems on the animal level (devolution for us), minus the quiet intercession of reason.

To get into this rat race, of course, you had to be excited to choose wrongly. Your forebears obliged you in this by feeding you lies that you accepted as true because of a latent egocentric propensity. Perhaps you believed that you were the perfect child of God and you resented those who did not pay you proper homage (rejected you). You judged them for this and resented them. You may still be spending most of your life energy on forcing them to give you your divine due (even though they might now have to give it to you from their graves). Either to judge or to accept praise is egotism, and puts our soul at war with our Creator. This is the sole reason for fear.

Those who live without discretion are simply extending what was passed on to them. They either enjoy their evil and wickedness or do not know how to get out of their rut. They may see the suffering they have caused, but simply do not know how to prevent themselves from inflicting it upon you or others. Your resentment of them involves you with them and causes you to follow suit. You will surely become just like them unless you find the way to stop resenting them. When you do, you may save them, as well as yourself, by not feeding back to them a reason to continue judging you in order to feel right about themselves. Seeing our weakness, we must cry inwardly for guidance.

THE FEAR DILEMMA: EXAMPLES

A man hated money because his father had pressured him with his wealth. His reaction was a foolish one. When he saw that he was trapped into being a failure—because he could not bear to be the glorious extension of his egotistical father—he became angry and tried to make himself like money. For him, this was as wrong as his former dislike. If he were to go back to his dislike for money, he couldn't live his life usefully; but to love it would make him become that which he hated—he had fear both ways.

A man made a fortune to compensate for his fear of poverty. When he reflected upon the way he had earned it, his conscience bothered him. So he gave it all away in an effort to redeem himself. Then, when he was poor again, and again hating his poverty, he was still afraid.

A man stole because of a parent's mishandling of a childhood indiscretion. Everyone was horrified, all upset, excited (delighted). He resented them. Now, if he doesn't steal, he will be like his hypocrite parents, wolves in sheep's clothing. By not stealing, he feels that he is conforming to that wicked hypocrisy. Rebelling (being "himself" by contrast), he wants to steal—but to do so makes him guilty and gives him more reason to fear. Never can he choose with reason—never is he free from two wrong alternatives.

A man becomes strong to compensate for his inferiority. So powerful does he become that he doesn't know his own strength when he is upset. Now, he is afraid to use that strength. When he does not use it, everyone takes advantage of his timidity. So he is afraid not only of his strength, but of people who might provoke him to use it—fearful of using it, and fearful of not using it.

Out of resentment, a young boy jumps into a pool to prove himself to his overly-protective mother. He almost drowns. Now he can't learn to swim because he is afraid. He directs his anger against the water, and because this is an unreasonable reply to stress, he becomes more fearful. He wants to overcome his fear, but he attempts to do so with resentment. Preoccupied with this dilemma, he forgets the original cause. He forgets that it all started with his resentment of his mother, that this resentment triggered the impulse to come face-to-face with a danger he was ill-equipped to face (having departed from reason by hating his mother). Through resentment of his mother's anxiety, he has made a fool of himself. Angered by his embarrassment, he begins a lifelong attack upon the water to save face, and is locked in mortal conflict—finding that he becomes more afraid in his angry determination. He can't learn to swim simply because it is prudent to do so; he is compelled to attack the water like a mad animal.

A man is called a fool by his mother. He becomes upset, showing that he has accepted the accusation. So painful is this to him that he works himself to the bone for ten years to make that mother "eat crow." She does. Being overwhelmed by indisputable evidence, she praises him and cancels her curse (for her own benefit). Now the man accepts another lie as the truth. He is not any better at all. If anything, he is worse. His first mistake was to be upset by another person's temptation; his second, to force that other person to pay homage to him. When he receives that praise, he becomes even more fearful. He discovers in himself a growing sensitivity to mean remarks, and a violent tendency to try to overcome others. He develops a fear of criticism and of the agony of laboring to prove himself to others (to offset suggestion). The sensitivity developed by accepting praise makes a person even more vulnerable to condemnation—there is fear both ways.

A child was beaten unconscious by her father because of an innocent remark she had made in regard to his weakness. Now she grows up afraid to speak the truth for fear of reexperiencing the terrible resentment she felt toward her father's brutality. But she is also afraid of a growing guilt feeling for failing to speak out. She knows that by remaining silent she is allowing all manner of evil to flourish around her.

We cannot prevail against evil by behaving in what only appears to be the opposite manner to what we become in our fall. This only keeps us revolving around the principle of evil. We can only truly overcome fear by finding innocence. Courage, poise and virtue appear when we discover how not to be upset by what confronts us. Through not dealing with our problem with resentment, we clear a way for the intercession of reason.

We are first tempted away from reason by unreasonable people, but we can end up by becoming afraid of any natural thing, such as thunderstorms, frogs, mice, spiders, etc. To compensate for the guilt of resentment and the fear it gives birth to, we go to unreasonable extremes. We fight in an effort to overcome our fear by trying to destroy the person or persons who caused our resentment in the first place. Or, becoming still more afraid, we may resign ourselves to our fate and retreat into a shell, only to discover that smaller things begin to be scary.

To attack any problem on the basis of being upset is to make a grave error; it ties us to that original sin. The person we resent is the very person who controls us, who determines what we shall be and what we shall do with our lives. We place the reins in his hands in the moment of our resentment.

Of ourselves, we cannot overcome fear and guilt, and as long as we are preoccupied with the egocentric effort to do so, we miss our real purpose in life—and become still more afraid. As long as we utilize the challenge provided by that wicked person in any way whatsoever, we shall never rest.

We will be afraid if we have money, or if we give it away.

We will be afraid of swimming; or if we become the best swimmer in the world, we shall be more afraid for having wasted our lives on the wrong goals (compensation), and for not doing what we should have done with our lives.

We will be miserable living like a thief, of living a respectable life—all because of resentment.

We will be insecure in poverty and in wealth.

We will be afraid of not conquering our fear, or conquering it—afraid to make a decision because it might bring us more reason to fear.

We have all made up our minds to "be" or "not to be" as the result of anger, which was the result of someone's injustice.

The breaking of our pattern of fear comes about by 1) realizing how wrong we are in the present, 2) relinquishing the resentment against the "cause" in the past, and 3) no longer making the conquest of symptoms an issue. The alternative to resentment is desiring anew to love. No more is necessary than to live each moment with grace, placing fairness first, because of our respect for what is good and because we are truly sorry for having fallen into temptation.

Of course, you cannot simply will these things to come about, so you must look to the meditation exercise to hold sway over your mind and flesh. Then one day, you will meet your old problems, and all those fears that come from frustration—and you will meet them fair and square.

Suddenly you are no longer afraid!

7

THE POWER OF LOVE

Emotional upset is the evidence of our failure to find love. Impatient, irritable individuals are easily influenced by stress in the wrong way. They absorb the problems of experience instead of the benefits. In resenting the weakness of others, they become the extension of the problem in those very people, for that is how those others became weak themselves.

The stimulation of hostility supports thought patterns, drawing the victim (through his responses) into the same patterns of error. By our hostile reactions, we take on the nature behind those very attitudes we resent when they are directed toward us. By overcoming such sensitivity, we react to injustice in a different way. We see what not to do, what to avoid—and by the same token, we also see what to be.

Through the implementation of the meditation exercise, that which we intuitively perceive becomes part of us and our natural way of life, causing us to shrink from the way of error. In other words, perceiving becomes a kind of positive direction to us, deconditioning our nature from its bondage to temptation and unreasonable demands. Life's cruelties then become a compost for new growth, rather than something to avoid.

When our awareness is undistorted by emotion, the way is obvious, in sharp contrast to the follies of the world. Awareness stimulates direction to our bodies, and we find the light of understanding shining upon our pathway through life, so that we no longer grope our way in darkness through the countless blind decisions of passion, feeling and emotion, pleasure-and-pain knowledge, excuses and analysis.

Pleasure and pain, liking and hating, are not opposite, as you might believe. One does not relieve the other. The pursuit of pleasure invariably brings pain—just as the pursuit of knowledge leaves us void of understanding. Because of this false concept, we reap bitterness.

When you manipulate others into liking you in order to keep from being upset, you arouse their larceny and end up by being abused by them—therefore upset just the same. And if you are bitter, ten thousand people can be nice to you and it can never cancel the anguish you feel. Kindness is quickly overlooked by the hate-filled consciousness, and one more cruel deed will affect it more than ten times ten thousand kindnesses.

Being nice to people to cheer them up can produce the opposite effect. The contrast between the bad they expect and have made a home for, and the good that you offer, for which they are unprepared, may increase the pain of their agony—so your efforts will go unrewarded, and this may cause a pain in you. Or, if they are not completely sealed off by bitterness, they may accept the comfort you offer— and promptly become dependent upon your "love" and take up all your time. This

132

too is painful and upsetting. Furthermore, they will come to resent their dependency on the comfort you provide, which should be coming from within themselves.

Possessed people occasionally seek relief by tempting others to correct them. Beware! Their hunger for correction sharpens their ability to distinguish between the true and the false, and great will be their resentment, their sense of elevation and judgment toward those who are stimulated to correct them or love them in the wrong way.

Hostility, although eventually painful, provides us with the drive to achieve our egocentric goals. It relieves lethargy and inflates the ego, giving it a glow of pride, providing the drive for success. Small wonder that proud people will not give up this seemingly valuable stimulation. Some people can move only when they are inspired to feel right, supported by praise, or angrily eager to show up another person by comparison. The anger makes them feel right in a wrong, pain-producing way.

Hate and pleasure are weird forms of the same thing. Hate, or resentment, provides the motivational drive. Excitement, pleasure and the approval of others encourage us to live from such motivation. So it is that we are often "loved" by others just as dishonest as we are. All this leads to greater pain and suffering which, when temporarily relieved by greater and greater pleasure, leads to more and more pain.

If you have been abused, it doesn't matter how many people are kind to you—they can never truly relieve the pain you feel. The only way you can be relieved of this accumulation of feeling is to discover how to stop responding resentfully to pressure. Resentment separates us from grace within and gives us a guilty conscience and pain. Excitement and pleasure further stimulate us away from virtue, causing more pain. Pleasure, not being a true remedy, is pain producing.

The opposite of "hate" is not "like." The opposite of hate is "not hate," also an impartial absence of emotion. The opposite of pain is not pleasure, but rather the joy of rightness, which comes out of not hating.

Joy and the conquest of pain are rooted in patience. This is love.

"Love (do not respond to) your enemy and do kindness to those who hate you," and "turn the other cheek" are simply ways of saying that non-response is our only true pain reliever (salvation).

When we allow ourselves to suffer cruelty without the pleasure of hostile reaction, to suffer discomfort without resentment, anger or impatience—without hating the pain— an entity other, and greater than, our ego is stressed and replies for us. This reply is a Godly pressure of growth in us and into the world about us. It projects a solution for our problems, as was the case with our former reactions. This is the proper way of meeting life, which, if practiced daily, will also reconcile past error. This new manner of living counteracts the reactions of past encounters that were handled inadequately and caused hurt in others.

To resent persecution and trial is to resent the Redeemer. For out of tribulation comes first the awareness of our lack, then pain, which leads to repentance and a new opportunity to live out of patience.

By running to pleasure to avoid pain, we hide from seeing our failing. How can we grow strong hiding from the knowledge of our weaknesses? How can we ever attain to virtue without correction in the face of temptation? How can we become brave without danger?

Anger is pride food. It makes us feel right when we are

not right. When we deny ourselves the luxury and emotional excitement of anger, we shall see our error, our guilt, and feel our shame.

When we judge others, we are distracted from the judgment upon ourselves for our past judgments. This is an egocentric relief that we enjoy, and, gorging ourselves on the substance of self-righteousness, we spoil our appetite for true love. This egocentric relief is a peculiar pleasure designed to relieve the pain of conscience. But after the excitement of the moment, we stand again more guilty.

Unrepentant before our conscience, we may rebel, do more of what is unwise, seek more approval to prove that we are free and right. This becomes self-punishment. We may try to relieve our guilt by doing greater mischief, inspired by our indignation against the requirements of our "enslaving" conscience and the pain of its correction. We come to hate ourselves. As the guilt increases with this process, we pridefully feel that our conscience is wrong for hurting us, so we may then strive to forgive ourselves in order to triumph over the conscience. But however much we try, that conscience remains ever above us in our guilty ways.

The fact that we lie and excuse ourselves is evidence of the truth about ourselves that we struggle a lifetime to deny so as to tread our own path and reach our own vain goals, supported by the stimulation of the world. The same motive leads us to seek the world's approval. We try to erase the effects of a guilty life by manipulating the affections of others.

Many of us confuse the meaning of the words "love," "like"and "need." When we marry for security, or to get away from home, or to escape loneliness—this is not love. This is need. Some marry for pure excitement, sex. This is like.

You can like ice cream,but you cannot love it. You can't

135

forgive or do kindness to an ice cream. In a more natural analogy, you need food, and you may like it too, but you still cannot love it.

You may need someone's affection to boost your ego, and you may like what you need, but you will also come to hate what you are dependent upon because when you need, you are not free.

Likewise, an angry man needs a drink to make him feel better, but when he drinks it he isn't better at all. He is worse off than he was prior to his compensation. Now he needs a larger drink, which he may believe that he likes because he needs it; yet he can also hate it for his unnatural dependency upon the need that enslaves him. His hate is the cause of his growing likes and needs. Because he hates what he needs, he is caused to need it more, to relieve the tension produced by his hate of it—and he likes it enough to come to hate it again.

Note carefully the following: you can like and hate at the same time. This frequently-observed phenomenon is called ambivalence. But you cannot love and hate at the same time. If you think that you do, it is because you think you love what you actually like, because you need it. We may "love" (like) members of the opposite sex, because they are more wrong than we are or because they are blind to our weakness.

Often we like those behind whom we can hide our weakness and thus appear right—we even marry them. We are strong in another's weakness, and we like this.

Love and patience keep you disenchanted from worldly madness, clear from the treadmill of pleasure and pain and "remedies" that lead to problems. Love preserves your inner unfoldment and prevents you from becoming as degenerate and bitter as your enemies. Love earns also the respect of your fellow seeker and disables the error in him, so that he may come to find within himself the virtue to be of genuine service to you too.

Like is the emotional response to the pleasant. Hate is the emotional response to the unpleasant. All of the pleasant sensations keep us from true love and sensitize us for a bigger negative response that we know as the letdown. Notice that both are emotional responses to things. Love, on the other hand, is original, and comes into being in spite of these two temptations. The evidence of love is the patient non-response of these two alien stimulations.

Quiet and unchanging as a rock, love cannot be altered, nor its tranquility disturbed, by pressure. It changes life by remaining unaffected by it. In love, we no longer live in the vicious cycle of moving to pleasure to offset pain, begetting in that pleasure more guilty pains as the result of our indiscretion.

Any fool can like others when they are nice, and any-one can hate people when they are bad, but there is no inner strength utilized here. A wrong person gives you reason to extend hatred or love, depending on how you look at it. Similarly, when someone wrong tempts you to like (approve of) them, it could instead be seen as cause to extend the un-moving correction of love. To like people unduly is to give them the approval they maneuvered for. It is to encourage them in their error, and thus to accrue error to yourself.

Wealthy or overly-sheltered people find it difficult to love (just as oppressed people find it difficult not to hate). Money brings protection from people and domination over them, instead of domination by them. If we are not stressed, we cannot demonstrate our love or see our failings.

Protected people have much applause and pleasure to compensate them for the tension and fear caused by their failure to love. Other unloving fools flatter the rich to obtain favors. How difficult it is for them to find their weaknesses while they are being bombarded with praises! Only through exposure to the experience of life can we see our failings and exercise love. Without trial, we cannot change and love cannot flower in us.

To become sensitive to what is right, and to champion (respond to) that rightness regardless of personal gain or loss, is loving—and unfolding from the truth. It is to become responsible.

A child who is caused to obey without emotional pressure discovers love. But if he conforms because of fear or bribery, he is weakened. If praise is the motivation, the child will grow up stupid, falsely believing that he is wise.

A wife who serves because she is afraid, or because she is moved secretly by hope for a favor, is not the same as the one who serves her husband freely, without any ulterior motives. And of course the same truth applies to the husband.

We need the strength to remind each other of our obligations without emotional pressure. The evidence of our love appears as this authority—to move others by reminding them of their true commitment. If we ourselves are not overcome by love, we cannot be patient and bring another to his own potential. In order to love another, we must first receive from God love's essence within ourselves. But our ego, being proud, rejects that inner pressure, refusing to be inferior and bound to unfold to a purpose other than its own. Such an ego, having rejected love at its source, has no love to extend to another.

Man's pride cannot allow him to receive graciously what God would bestow upon him in secret. Instead, it insists that he must occupy the exalted place himself, and have evidence of his worthiness offered up to him from other men and women below. Pride is a thief. It steals men's attention away from their own true selves.

Doing things in love is different from doing things for a calculated effect or for profit. When our intent is wrong we are frustrated, whether we do or do not receive what we maneuvered to get. When we "love" others out of such a wrong intent, and the love is not returned, we feel that we are being drained dry—we give and give and give and nothing happens. In other words, our giving is not really giving, because we expected something back—and we are not getting it. If it should happen that our "love" is returned, we may feel guiltier than ever for having hoodwinked our innocent victim.

Love originates from within—not from another person!

If you have to be pressured to manifest love, it is not love that you manifest. Indeed, anything you manifest as the result of pressure lacks integrity. The little boy who does his homework from a sense of responsibility learns better than the boy who is nagged into doing his homework. Although both boys labor, only one of them will really learn correctly. The other will become a clever robot, able to move only when he is pressured. Or he can become so rebellious to the injustice of emotional pressure that he cannot learn at all. Eventually he may become afraid of the knowledge that only confuses him.

That is why you must be conscientiously attentive to the inward intuitive guidance through using the meditation exercise. With it, you can draw the strength to love, to be patient from the heart—not with pretense, not just with the outward appearance.

True love is the most important discovery you can make. The journey begins when we discover that we are incapable of originating love, and that we have lived separated from it through our acceptance of the adoration of fools. Any emotional experience that imparts to us a sense of rightness, varying from the love of others to our judgment upon them, keeps us apart from truth and makes us part of the hypocrisy of the world.

A consciousness that fails to stabilize the body through gentle inward pressure leaves it at the mercy of conditions, easily influenced by pleasure or pain, like or dislike, easily programmed by the ugliness residing in society. Love affects conditions through not being tempted by them. There is no conflict involved here—for to a whole person, temptation has nothing to offer.

Disturbed people do not live out of inner wisdom. Their ideas, words, feelings and actions are stimulated by the conditions and emotions in the environment.

Because we are empty of love, we resort to getting others to like us, so that we can lift ourselves by the playback of their feelings. But no one can love truly if he seeks out and lives on the approval of others or waits for their encouragement to spur him into activity.

We become slaves when we depend upon spouse, parent or friend to give us approval. When we become aware of our bondage, we are horrified to see our "greatness" turn into inferiority. Then begins the struggle to topple the balance and enslave our masters. Secretly defeated, we may falsely believe that if we give in to avoid argument we are good. We may even discover the wicked art of giving in quickly to our opponent's demand so that he doesn't want it any more. Generally speaking, giving in is trading true principles for peace. But he who trades in that way cannot gain real peace of mind, love or goodness. Being egocentric, we must labor for the good *feelings* which substitute for virtue. This illusion is the candy that spoils our appetite for what is truly good.

When we become victims of pressure, decisive action becomes more and more impossible, for the law of life demands that we bring forth what we have or lose it altogether. Standing firm in our awareness of what is wise each moment, with patience, develops a tenacity to face any consequence and gives us the foundation we need to meet greater problems.

Patience is the unwavering persistence that comes through perceiving the importance of virtue. It is courageous, the substance of decision; it is the evidence and the outcome of faith. Courage separates us from other people, exposing us to criticism for our truthfulness (which awakens and pains them), but thereby also gives us greater opportunity to exercise our strength in love.

True love is dispassionate—yet compassionate. It is not something you feel good about. The first phase of love is emotional non-response to the unkindness of those around us, especially relatives and friends. The second phase lies in the timing of our words and actions toward others.

We naturally expect our relatives to be kind to us, but since they are "only human," they are bound to inflict some injustice upon us sooner or later. When this happens, it is time to love, to be patient and to remain calm. Then, when things change for the better, we shall enjoy a better relationship than before. They will respect us for the unjudging, correcting nature that does not encourage or feed off of their wrongs.

Of course, you should not labor to like offensive people in order to offset the pain of your resentment toward them. Forcing yourself to like unrespectable persons, you license them for more error. They will provoke you again, making it necessary for you to like them again—until you can't stand it any more. Eventually, you get fed up—with them, you think, but it's really your own hypocrisy that sickens you.

Liking, perhaps, should be reserved for things, not people. When you like people, you condone them and encourage them toward error. By disliking them, on the other hand, you judge them and compel them toward error.

Love, by its very nature, is incompatible with liking and disliking. You cannot love and like the same person at the same moment, any more than you can love and dislike the same person at the same moment. You can, however, love and respect the same person at the same time. When you like another, you are invariably blinded to his faults by your emotional need for his admiration—then begins the tragedy of emotional attachment.

Love is not emotional and it is never an attachment. It is exercised in the face of persecution and temptation, and that includes the temptation to like or to hate, to be selfish or overkind, in order to build up your own ego.

"Love your enemy and do kindness to those who hate you" is another way of saying the same thing. To love your enemy is to be patient with him. And to do kindness is the extension of that love toward those unlikeable persons who tempt you to hate or "like" yourself into the pain of judgment.

The more we respond to this inner principle, the more it controls our mind and life. The observation of the outcome of love brings wisdom. A person who is illumined by love has confidence and understanding—we see him as being "his own man."

When we allow our egocentric need for people or things to become our controlling factor, we become chained to wrong kinds of people—ironically, those we hate the most. Those who tempt us lure us away from our inner nature by offering us what we ought never to have desired.

Love and understanding come from the inside out. To emulate the outer bearing of a saint will never make us saintly. And these words, though they express my understanding, can only be outer knowledge to you. You must see with your own eyes, and look within yourself for the reality they bear witness to.

The ancient laws given to Moses were truths engraved upon a stone. These truths were obeyed (for the most part) because of the pressures society brought to bear out of its need to survive. These laws were a necessary part of the evolution of mankind. Before they arrived on the scene, people used ignorance as an excuse for their errors. The presence of these laws brought guilt upon us all. They were the evidence of what each one, ambitious in his own way, had secretly denied. Yet the following of these laws did not help the children of Israel, as the Good Book showed. For when Moses' back was turned, they reverted to their old "free" egocentric ways. These laws were followed largely through the shock of fear— the true principles were not yet written into the heart and mind of man.

Outer direction and laws written upon books are not the same as truth engraved upon the mind from within. Conformity to law does not bring salvation. Enforced goodness is not the same as virtue. When you do good or obey laws because you are supposed to, or to ease guilty feelings, or to get something in return, you are wasting your time. The wrong motive poisons everything you do. Emotional pressure cannot make you good. Laws cannot save you; they only temporarily restrain people from violating one another.

The secret of living properly lies in the motivation behind our practice of the commandments, and—most important— the way in which they enter our mind. Without the humility to receive, and meditation to implement, the ectoplasm of truth into our nature, our actions are meaningless and empty. We are puppets pulled by an outer "conscience," filling our emptiness with the empty pleasures, material things and the noise of knowledge. Only the letter of the law is carried out, usually with the same obligated reluctance as that with which we lend our lawnmower or give to charity. We study truth only to use it as a weapon of power, to give us the appearance of being right, to hide our evil aims, or to build up our sense of being good.

Often the learning of Scripture is only for the purpose of feeding ourselves a sense of goodness that is not at all good and that gives rise to a growing compulsion, an unholy need, to study the word. Without love, the letter kills us. Only the Spirit gives us life.

The secret lies in our hunger and thirst for righteousness, through which understanding is revealed, not studied. The concentration of the meditation exercise causes the word to enter into the heart and mind, set in motion from within. Responding to it, we see the essence of truth in its reality. We become mindful of the delicate requirements of each moment. Our love of goodness brings that truth into view and our meditation implements its physical expression each moment, touching the hearts of all men and women.

With a full understanding of principle, we realize that no one can hurt those who are perfect in love. Acts of unkindness and abuse only serve as opportunities to develop, through action, that which would otherwise not exist.

Love works through the exercise of patience. To find love, you must give up your personal ambitions and give first place to justice and fairness for each moment. To see truth again, you must desire to serve good and bear witness to right, and stop trying to appear to be that right.

As you meditate, examine each thought, impulse and action. Note whether or not you are desiring to accomplish something to satisfy your egocentric self. Every "kind" action that is designed to bring back a profit—prestige, respect, money, glory, riches, honor and the like—can bring only frustration. It is wrong to be kind for some value to yourself. This is not kindness at all!

It is also unwise to try to prove yourself to others. The desire to do so indicates that you have been offended by their judgment, when you should not have been affected by them at all. Everything you do that is motivated by a desire to build up your ego image must necessarily hurt other people as well as your own self. It means that somehow you have fallen. Your real need is not for ego support, but for inner calmness and patience so that you will not be affected by praise or criticism. What you have lost through being upset cannot be regained by compensation or the support of others. Your friends cannot make you right, nor can you make yourself right, even though your friends may assure you that you have already done so. Nor can you be a better person by elevating yourself over others by any means. The person who needs to look right is obviously wrong.

If we make others believe that we are right, we must necessarily deceive them and blind them to what is truly right. If they give us praise, they do so as the result of our manipulation of their minds. If they say we are good, it is because they have lost sight of real good—and if we believe them, we are welcoming back our own lie and deceiving ourselves as well as them. When we use our friends in this way to build up our image, we are like the vain woman who simpers and flirts with her reflection in the mirror.

The opinions of others should never have had the power to excite us in the first place. We must stop struggling for the "love" of others, stop hungering for their approval. If we accept a lie as a truth, we become more wrong, even hungrier for the admiration that will destroy our real values and replace them with an illusion of worth.

Long ago, a weakness was revealed in us. Our ego was tempted by a parent's failure to correct us with love. Resentfully, we wasted our time seeking that "love" from others—failing that, we sought compensation by elevating ourselves over them. This is the cause of all our troubles.

What we do to perpetuate our own sense of good is an evil, both to those we deceive (through our cunning) into adoring us and to ourselves, for accepting their acclaim, emotional confusion and errors as evidence of our correctness. The good that we do for our own sense of worth is always frustrating, and not really good. It weakens others to "love" us, and weakens us to need that unsatisfying love. Love that is a growing need is not love.

We can relate to another person correctly only if we do not need to love, or to be loved—respect and real love flower only if the relationship is a right and reasonable association of two persons. Therefore, do not secretly obligate others or expect anything for your good deeds. Courtesy should always be offered without strings, because it is the natural thing to do—not because you have to, nor for any calculated return.

Be sure your love does not smother or disable another. If you are to enjoy receiving from others, be sure that you help their own grace to function by that receiving.

The antidote to unhappiness is not pleasure or enjoyment. It is more patience. It is the resolving of anger in the presence of stress. It is a somewhat indifferent attitude in that you do not care with your feelings, but you do care with your understanding. For instance, if you give in to a nagging child because you can't stand his crying, your attitude toward the child is one of selfishness; your "kindly" decision is for the relief of your own nervousness, not for the true benefit of the child.

When you are patient, you maintain a detached attitude. Thus you are able to perceive when someone has a real need that should be met and when he is only trying to influence you by his nagging. By being patient and not giving in to him, you demonstrate that anger brings him nothing. You enable your love to disable his craving, your reason to cancel his folly, in order that he may respect your reason and, by virtue of shame, find salvation. Simply to respect the appearance of virtue in another is to welcome that same virtue in ourselves. By learning to be calm, you will lean more and more toward what is wise, instead of living at the beck and call of your emotions. This is true love.

By your demonstration of patience, you will bear witness to the principles which others have forgotten. You will find that certain people will respect this kind of strength and cease to take advantage of you. You can do much more for your loved ones when you are not so emotionally upset and involved with them. Furthermore, you discourage them from the ways of error and weakness by this real strength. This practice contributes to their progress as well as to your own well-being.

Have you ever noticed that when you really like others, either they take advantage of you or you drive them away? Liking is a token of judgment on their goodness, for which they may like you into supporting your own sense of goodness. Eventually, their growing moral weakness will be revealed and they will take advantage of your growing need for them. When you demonstrate your need, you thereby reveal the incompleteness of your love; for, as we previously discussed, need is not love.

Don't misunderstand. Be kind. Be patient. Do kind things in a kindly way, because you want to. In this way, you demonstrate that you are strong and full of love. This effortless grace is quite opposite from drudgery. It is also quite different from appeasing and being appeased, or serving in growing anxiety lest the favors be not returned to you, or suffering frustration, both in gaining "love" and in being denied that false love. Be sure that your actions are not motivated by the desire to gain favor or approval from others, and others will respect you more. Also, by this display of strength, you will find yourself attracting more wholesome friends.

Allow me to elaborate so that you may better understand. When you are devoid of love yourself, you have need. When nothing satisfies that need, you are frustrated. Pressure builds up through frustration, which makes you renew your efforts to gain the "love" of others to satisfy your needs; but that "love," once gained, is upsetting, disgusting, or guilt-producing.

Now your enemies will try to tempt you to take advantage of your needs. Aware of your weakness of giving in so as to stay calm, they will praise you and weaken you to need them. They know that you will do anything to avoid being upset, to gain approval and preserve your self-image, and that you will therefore lend yourself to gratifying their perverted designs on you. To you, because you are doing so much to relieve pressure, it appears that you always seem to love those who hurt you the most. But in reality we always serve those we hate the most and, because we feel ennobled by that service, we call the relationship "love."

148

The meditation exercise eliminates these mental gymnastics, and through your not-responding you will remain calm under stressful conditions, without the need to give in. Notice that you will see nothing in this text except what you are ready to see via an inner growth process. For the knowledge recorded here becomes clear primarily through your observation of what is occurring in you.

If your consciousness loves what is right, you will naturally desire to forfeit selfish advantage. Because of that true desire, you will see in each moment what to do. As long as you can see what is right, you will spurn temptation that once seemed to promise good, and you will make no errors of discernment. By giving up the stimulations and excitements, judgments and praises of the world, you will allow an unfoldment of purpose in you. What will appear in you to others as calmness will be the result of an inner excitement.

You may also notice that you are accomplishing more now in less time, and whereas your hours and days once seemed to drag, they now seem to pass quickly. This is because your meditation changes the relationship between you and time, and you are relieved of the former meaningless drudgery of relieving your unhappiness in unhappy ways.

Do not be impatient with your own unfoldment. Wait and watch. Do not be impatient to arrive at a greater understanding than you are ready for. Don't try to force your new insights and understandings upon others. Wait for them to come to you as a result of their wonder and respect for your growing strength.

By growing to understand these truths, you will begin to believe more in yourself. These words merely bear witness to what is already waiting to unfold from within. To acknowledge these truths with gladness is to love the Maker of truth. You are saved by desiring to see truly, and by acknowledging the falseness of your former way of life in the light of your new understanding. By this understanding you will have faith. You will be responsive to inward urgings and will draw closer to reality and a purpose that has been prepared for you.

Do not add anything to these meditations, nor take anything away, for the understanding you now possess will always be available within you, provided you continue to do your exercise.

Patience is the evidence of your first reaction to common sense, and it allows you to see clearly without emotion the next correct thing to do or say. Remember, because tolerance and love are becoming the natural, effortless motivations in your daily life, you will be able to make the right decision with ease at the right time—and the greatest of these decisions is to overlook immediately and be outspoken, with firmness, kindness and patience, or to overlook and say nothing, depending on the situation.

Always act out of what you know is just for each moment. When you put aside all thought of consequences, right action brings about a chain of events that will lead you beyond all limitations, bringing to you all the material things, such as health and abundance, that you once ambitiously labored for in vain. Remember, love what is right first, and all other things come as a matter of course—you have no need for anxiety. Remember also that you may be in your present occupation, frustrating though it may be, for a purpose you have not yet recognized. Do not then utilize your natural talents to glorify yourself and to compensate for the prestige that your occupation lacks.

The veil over understanding the very Bible you read will fall away and you will begin to perceive truth in all its glory

150

and splendor. You no longer have to grope your way through life, easing your pain; rather, everything you do will be in the clear light.

You will find that you can still think of other things, but always in relation to truth, guiding you and conditioning the way you will react to life each moment, giving you a subtle sense of joy in each moment of each success with principle.

Anger, fear and intellect are not your protection. Understanding, or non-reactive love, is your armor for life. Face the danger before you without fear or anger, without dealing with it from your own ego. Be aware of the pains of your various problems, and the Spirit of truth will be stressed to reply for you.

8

SELF-RELIANCE

When we are faced with the choice between what is right, just and fair, and what seems to be most advantageous and profitable, nearly all of us choose the apparent gain. This is our second departure from reality.

The first departure occurred when our parents praised and/ or upset us out of our common sense, tempting our egos and feeding us the emotional food of pride and judgment. When we could no longer see clearly how things really were, a mist of excuses arose, which veiled our mind. These excuses became our thoughts, forming the foundation for our next action and leading to bad decisions and frustration.

Meanwhile, the breach in our consciousness remained open, rendering us subject to more of the same phenomena. The first mistake leads to conflict, which leads to the excuse to remedy the conflict. When the excuse seems to become the truth, we then have confusion. We do not recognize this process because we have excused it so cleverly. We excuse it because we do not want to see our failings, and we do not want to see our failings because of our proud and self-seeking nature.

We are proud if we have chosen to continue to defy what is right. A proud, ambitious person cannot receive. He must take. But grace can only be received—it cannot be taken by storm and force. Grace is correction; grace is love. When through selfishness we err, we refuse to see the wrong we have incurred and we argue against correction. This is pride, and pride defends (justifies) the wrong, and it hates the right.

When we choose a life of ambition and self-created purpose, we deny the pressure toward potential goodness which conscience provides. At that moment, deep down inside us, there is an imperceptible motion away from the unfoldment that is prepared for us and that would have kept us whole and virtuous had we chosen to unfold obediently to God. At this moment, too, there is an attraction to the substance of the lie. And so we are cleaved away from the truth in our conscience by excitement. Having rejected the path of truth, we prefer to be inspired by the voice that promises to uphold our secret ambition, offering us its apparent benefit. The first day we responded to the tempter who perceived our weakness was the first day of our downfall. But now that we have become egocentric, we have forgotten that day of long ago. We have excused and covered our weakness for so long that the excuse has become our pattern of righteousness.

Ladies and gentlemen, we are wrong, and we do not recognize our error. There may be a prickling in our conscience, or a hollow in our soul, but we hurry to remedy the pain of our failing and to fill our emptiness. We do it through being excited by the weaknesses and errors of others; we call this excitement love and hate. Soon we find our-

154

selves becoming easily upset over trivial matters, or craving approval. We need excitement because we need its pressure to move, to substitute for and to countermand the obligation of the inner pressure.

Hostility charges us up with excitement over another's injustice. In this puffing up, which fills us with a sense of rightness, we feel a sadistic satisfaction which dulls our perception of the judgment that comes upon ourselves from within. The excitement of seeing someone else's error drowns out the condemnation we feel upon ourselves. It provides us with the energy we need to feel guiltless about our failures and selfish projects.

Again, this is another wrong! Soon we feel the aftermath of our mistakes and our judgment upon others; again we feel that hollow in our soul, and beyond that hollow, the silent voice of conscience. Egocentrically feeling this judgment upon ourselves, we judge the judgment and embrace damnation.

We think to ourselves, "If I had something to drink... if I had someone to love me...if only I had something very exciting to make me forget...if...if...if..."

Excitement feels like salvation. But the very remedy we need interferes with the achievement of our personal ambitions and goals. It is never satisfying, and it is a greater wrong. We never intended to be the world's greatest drunk, of course—or glutton, or chainsmoker.

After the stimulation has subsided, we feel remorse because of our greater error. Then we are angry and frustrated at our failure to remedy our fault—we become even more determined and vow to make our remedy work. We feel guilty for not going to church, and even more guilty for not offsetting our guilt with more of the excitement that we embrace as "right." "If I had another this…or more of that," we say. "I can't stop! Woe is me! I can't make it gratify! Oh, how my thirst for everything grows, and yet I can never quench it."

It is the same with the love we need from others to support our faltering ego. We need the applause from others to drown out that same sense of shame and fear, but this is wrong! We become hungrier and hungrier, yet the hollow is never filled.

We even feel guilty for not embracing the error that seems to offer salvation. Now we exist only to prove our righteousness to ourselves through the love and admiration of others and through smoke screens of pleasure.

Finally, when all this fails to satisfy us, we then delight in torturing those who refuse to see our righteousness. We weaken them to make them dependent, and we must mistake this dependency as evidence of their love for us. This "love" we interpret as their approval of our righteousness, and so it goes. We now become dependent on their dependency, the false love that never satisfies. And they now cling to us for some piteous approval of their own wrong. We too are depending upon the approval they are forced to give us by virtue of our having disabled them by various means; or, perhaps, they become disgusted with our vampiric nature and flee from us. This is our chance to make ourselves seem right by condemning them!

Always, we are screened from seeing our own weakness by the seemingly greater faults of others. Always, we seek those devices by which we can dull our conscience with pleasures and the adoration or condemnation of other sinners. How glad we are that nobody is perfect, lest they should reveal our fiendish soul to us!

This is the meaning of addiction of all kinds: a growing appetite for pleasure and applause, which will uphold our "right" in the face of reality, but which is in itself a greater wrong…which makes a bigger vacuum and a bigger appetite that can never be filled or satisfied.

Even though many of us do not consciously embrace and live by the delicate principles of wisdom, we become angry at the indiscretions of other people, revealing that we do, after all, have some awareness of truth—how else could we judge? Usually, the error we are judging in others is one that is presently residing in ourselves. We seek to escape the condemnation we feel inwardly by crucifying another for that same fault. Thus, all eyes are focused upon another's weakness, and away from our own.

But isn't this precisely the trick that led to our own bitterness? Were we not also once accused of the very faults possessed by an accuser? How did we react? How did we escape from the force of those terrible suggestions? One's first impulse is usually to become upset and shout louder than the accuser, trying to excite the suggestion back into him. This invariably fails, because the accuser has the power advantage of seniority, having already put you on the defensive by upsetting you.

If we become violent and rebel, we become worse than the accuser, relieving him of his own guilt. If we accept the accusation, we spend our lives trying to rid ourselves of a particular fault that does not truly belong to us, but to another. Guilty we are, indeed! But only because we have foolishly taken upon ourselves the guilts of others, giving them power, freeing them to wallow uncorrected in their loathsome ways.

The seeds of all bad habits germinate in the soil of our foolish response to temptation and torment. For example, if I accuse you, and you resent my accusation, a strange evolution of cause and effect takes place in your nature. It is all variations on a theme, a complicated struggle to offset the effects of your emotional feelings. When you are upset or excited, you fail to handle a situation with patience and discretion. As I have stated elsewhere, impatience is the point of departure from our relativity with the Unchanging Good. This is our first wrong, and from it, all our other faults proceed.

How can you make a liar, or a false accuser, see the error of his ways? The answer is fairly obvious. You can never make him see his own mistake. His reason for accusing you is to escape from observing that same error in himself, through judging your judgment. He does not want you to improve. The object of his criticism is not to make you into a better person, for if he were to succeed in this, the contrast between you would force him to see his own weakness. People are often heard moaning, "If he would be all right, I would be all right!" God forbid they should be all right!

The object of most ridicule and criticism is to upset you away from an inner standard in order to cut down any contrast of betterness. People live by their evaluation of others, while providing others fuel for evaluation of them. The accuser tries to impart to you the notion that you have a certain fault, and even though you may not possess such a fault at that moment, you soon will, if you are upset. Being upset can make you pick up the suggestion of another person. It is a subtle hypnosis that mesmerizes you away from yourself.

This is when you feel guilty, but not of the thing of which you have been accused. Rather, it is for being excited over the lie, for becoming angry (or, in a different situation, puffing up in acceptance of false praise), and failing to hold fast to what you know in your heart.

Anger or resentment arises when an ego responds defensively, indignantly, to not being seen in a good light and given the proper homage. The anger excites us away from our center, and we become increasingly susceptible to suggestion. Now we labor for those effects (respect, homage), and failing that, we labor to get above those who are denying them to us. But that "aboveness" is also the cause of our suffering. It is, in fact, our real guilt, and the reason for our growing sense of inadequacy, though we falsely associate our uneasiness with statements and opinions about us expressed by others.

Now, having set out to prove that we are right, we can do so only by proving that others are wrong. But proving them wrong does not, and never can, make us truly right.

Suppose someone is right in his criticism of our fault. Will it make us right to prove him wrong? Of course not. We are more wrong for believing it to be the case, and we grow more proud and self-deceived all the while.

Shall we be relieved of our guilt (for our departure from reality) by proving another person wrong? What I mean is, will it mend a broken inward relationship? Surely the effort to make another wrong, in order to reinstate our own sense of rightness, is always another wrong. Conversely, does the approval of another ever make us right?

The approval of another person, or his humiliation—isn't this what we all waste our labors upon? Surely, seeking approval from another in order to prove our worthiness, or to earn forgiveness, is an utter waste of time and life. It is only a motion toward greater guilt, which we again unfortunately associate with an original accusation made upon us.

Can you really satisfy an accuser? I think not. Your labor is to get above him. You labor for his approval, and this entrenches him more deeply in false righteousness. Your own labor makes you feel even more guilty and hopeless, and again you associate the feeling with accusation.

Now, because of all the frustration that grows up in you, you long for relief. Usually you end up with the sin that you resented being accused of, enjoying its pleasure, since you have already suffered the punishment. When an idea is constantly on your mind (put there by excitement), it must eventually find expression.

When you labor to offset another person's bad impression of you, you are merely laboring to ease the effects of the outside world upon you. But does approval (if and when you receive it) cancel out the original disapproval?

The person who elevates you by encouragement and lifts your spirits is as cruel as the one who deflates and discourages you. You lost your inner support, self-reliance, and belief in yourself in the first place through being excited. You cannot reclaim virtue by getting other people to make some opposite observations of you, because this too is an excitement which weakens your mind and makes you susceptible to more negative impressions. This, in turn, makes you labor once more for relief through that same futile cycle which leads only to agony and perhaps finally, resignation to your accuser's judgment upon you.

When we believe the lie, what then do we doubt? Is it not that which we once knew was truly right? It is God's grace that keeps calling to us through conscience, and it is He whom we doubt and try to crucify.

Once we are caught up in the lie, self-reliance is impossible to us, for we have lost contact with that "Self" that would have been our refuge and our strength, had we chosen to submit to its direction. Now, we must necessarily take our stand on the shifting sands of relative value and comparative virtue, and we wear ourselves out trying to impress others with a strength that we do not have.

We are only as strong as that which we stand next to, that from which we draw our strength, and as surely as love will always triumph over hate, truth will ever be stronger than the lie. In the strict sense, of course, we cannot be the source of that strength, that love, that truth—but when we submit to their dominion, we, the created beings, bear witness to God who created us and who could have us clothed in His virtues. We are filled from within; joy runs over. When we see another's true need, we have something to extend to him.

A person who feels the pressure of obligation moves in a different orbit from the one who gives simply because he wishes to give. When we agree to anything reluctantly (pressured by fear of consequences), or over-obligingly (because another's apparent need is great), puppet-like responses will extend into other situations. We "give 'til it hurts," and in these circumstances, any giving hurts, but we don't know how to stop.

The person who can agree to lend or give with graciousness can also say "no" graciously. Denying, lending, or giving—and doing it with dignity—sets in motion a different and healthier chain of events in other relationships, affecting not only our own lives but also those we touch.

The resentful giver is a slave without a will of his own, always striving to please or yielding to get everyone "off his back." Yet he may not see his slavery, as his egocentric self-image is upheld by his own observation of the many "good" things he is forced to do. He never lives his own life; he justifies his weakness; he observes his great sacrifices—and he calls this "loving too much"!

Without knowledge of self-motivation, we all feel embarrassed by our lazy, selfish ways, so we need pressure to hide this feeling of inadequacy from ourselves. Under pressure, then, we may wind up behaving in a seemingly kind and concerned manner, but it exerts a different effect upon our health, sanity, and social affairs than the truly unselfish motivation would. The person who stops at the traffic light because he doesn't want to hurt another is quite a different breed from the man who stops because he is afraid of receiving a traffic citation. They are each operating under a different principle. Only the outward appearance is the same. When the pressure of the law is removed, the action of the first person remains the same, whereas the second person reveals his lawless, unprincipled nature. An individual who is led by the love of right encounters a completely different set of experiences from those of the man who is merely afraid to be bad.

Many people appear to be honest only because they are afraid to be dishonest, or because they seek to gain from their brand of honesty. The pressure that would stimulate one person would leave another unmoved. Though their outward behavior might appear to be identical, the effect each would have on his surroundings would be utterly different.

For example, many maneuver egocentrically to obligate you to give; then, excited by your compulsive giving, they come back for more and more. Even under these circumstances, if you were correct, you could give from grace, overlooking the pressure. The conniving person might then feel guilty for receiving, and either be corrected or frightened away.

The motive behind any decision is the key to the positive or negative reaction to that decision. The obliging fool may be found serving society, but his service is a drudgery and enslavement, and not the extension of his own talent for good. When an egotist is cut off from true values, he often seeks a sense of values by helping all the strays and feeling sorry for them. Here, his words and actions seek out support for his dwindling self-image and his own advantage. Motivated by his growing need to feel superior and to appear good by helping everyone, he becomes a slave of the mood of others, whom he must waste his life attending. Of course, no one is really being aided. The recipients of such largesse are only encouraged in their idleness; they enjoy their new slave who is excited to aid them more and more.

The need for motivation is the evidence of our failing. The pressure of experience places us in the position of choosing between sense and sensation. When we are correct, we act out of a deep stirring from within. Lacking this inner motivation, we need pressure for a facsimile of correctness.

Each time you are stressed is an opportunity to express your true identity, and each moment of truth will bear the likeness of that nature. You are either servants of the Most High, or you are slaves of the hell in each other.

The proper exercise of principle enables you to grow and brings with it various fringe benefits of confidence and self-reliance. That is why it is important to keep on practicing the meditation exercise for the right reason. If you stop, you will fall back into your old ways again, and then you may return to the exercise because you are afraid not to. Your agony then takes precedence over good purpose and preoccupies your mind with seeking to *feel* better instead of being better. Meditation under these circumstances becomes an addiction. You may be meditating—but meditating out of fear can cause confusion and terror, even oblivion.

You must meditate because you want to be a better person, not because you are afraid of the consequences of your failure to do so. Willingness and fear are two different drives, different and diametrically opposed. Both may result in the same "right"action, but with opposite effects. The exercise is done to allow the expression for right, not for any feeling of pleasure or relief that can be obtained from it. The secret of the exercise is that it makes us the same on the inside as we often pretend to be on the outside.

We often feel a conflict between two opposing ways; we do not feel right about doing right. To resolve this conflict, we may decide that living the wicked life would be more honest, but we are not happy going this way either.

Meditation gives us the strength to stand up for what is clear to us, without the need for pressures. It does not allow emotional conflict to develop. It allows us to express our true selves, and to extend good.

You see, no emotional response to the outside can be good or positive. What we express as the result of outer pressure hurts others, and what we keep to ourselves hurts us from within. Most of us live solely to support a sense of worth about ourselves. The good things we do arise out of a growing need to puff up our pride. If we were right, we would not need to feel good about what we do. We would need neither appreciation nor praise. If we do have these needs, we are dependent upon those who feed them. The rightness we feel is wrongness, and the freedom we feel is slavery. The praise of others is our humiliation.

Even if we do a good deed, we may not feel good about it. This tends to increase our craving for appreciation. We need it to countermand the guilt feelings that arise in us when we accept praise. Our ego is lifted up in the wrong manner and our higher self is blocked. In the same light, we must not do creative work merely to glorify ourselves. As a matter of fact, if we can look on any work that we do as "creative," we are self-deceived, as there is but one Creator, one God, one Source of all that is good. If we do look on what we have done as creative, we are filled with an artificial self-valuation which both blocks out true industriousness and causes dissipation in our expression. Now, more needful of motivation from the excitement of achievement, we are compelled again and again to relieve our lethargy and the guilt feelings that arise when we are idle. We feel guilty for not "creating," and we are guilty when we do. This is a vicious cycle that never ends.

A person who is ambitious is impatient, needful of energy, and is easily swayed by conditions or directions from others. Our wrong intent disqualifies us from the energy excited by perception of reason, and causes the need for emotion that expresses as impatience. What we do, aided by that emotion, bears the mark of our egocentric ways.

The meditation exercise you have learned is the communication with the real life. The exercise rekindles the response to conscience. What shall be revealed through the practice of patience makes possible the giving up of our personal ambition. Pride and ambition are the root of all wrong. Patience allows virtue by eliminating reaction to external conditions. The tranquility gained in the exercise is carried over into our daily lives, so that we make decisions in calmness, for the right reasons. If you need excitement to accomplish anything, it follows that it cannot be right.

The first common sense action is patience, which allows the second common sense pattern to appear. If we have enough control to be patient, then we have enough control to bring forth what then appears as reason.

Self-reliance is confidence in the wisdom arising within the framework of our consciousness. It implies a dependency relationship between the response and what is perceived.

Self-reliance, in other words, is a dependence; but it is a dependence on the inside, not the outside, world. It is a true in-dependence.

Pride causes us to pursue false goals and promises, and then it needs to ease the pain of goal-reaching that always fails to bring happiness. It is injured when we fail to make good our promises to ourselves, and when we lose faith in our ability to do so, we call it losing confidence.

Any motivation or encouragement that is provided by others is as bad as, if not worse than, discouragement. Either one is a stimulus to our pride. Eventually, we will feel guilty about enjoying our comforts, encouragements and pleasures—as frustrated and guilty as we would have been, had we failed to attain them. We are afraid to fail, because our ego loses face; but we can become just as afraid of success, because of the guilt it induces in us. Fear of success can become converted to an enervating and subtle stimulation to our pride—we, having nothing, look down upon the unscrupulous ones who are grubbing in their ill-gotten gains.

If your mind is in the dark, your whole body is in darkness. Understanding is the foundation of inner direction and life. Without this, your nature gropes in the dark. You become a ship without a rudder, influenced by everyone, everything, and every mood. To have the gift of understanding, you must love what is right—and you must seek first and above all to know the purpose for living, not to get what you want out of life.

The ostrich, growing fat and awkward, neglected to use his wings and so lost his ability to fly. To compensate, he developed stronger legs. Unaware of the laws by which he was governed, he nevertheless lived in obedience to them, and now he cannot fly.

The light which humility brings forth will illumine our way and thereby save us. If we do not bring it forth, it is taken away, and we will perish for lack of it. Nothing can compensate for this loss. Compensation is only an illusion for the fool who seeks to appear right in his folly. But we do try to compensate, don't we? And so we lose our "wings," and become graceless clumsy oafs.

No form of outer assistance can substitute for inner direction. Direction must come always from within. Moved by the spirit of intuition, we live without excitement, effort, or strain. The more we exercise our dependency upon what comes from within, the stronger this relationship becomes, and we know it as grace.

Should you use devices or people as aids to self-conditioning, you will become dependent on them. And every form of addiction, from drugs to needing people, is the reverse of self-reliance; it is outside-world reliance.

No matter how many times "positive-thinking" books, affirmations, teachers, or recorded voices assure you that you are strong, brave, confident, healthy, and happy in your own egocentric self, it will be a lie, because you are depending upon them to tell you something that can never be, except in illusion. There may be short periods of apparent gain, but while you are distracted from your suffering, unsuspected dissipation will be taking place under the surface with each session.

Encouragement is not the opposite of discouragement. It simply weakens you, rendering you dependent upon the embrace of "love" from others. But when trial and tribulation come, and you are not rooted within yourself, great is your confusion and powerlessness.

Self-confidence, courage, wisdom and all the fruits of the Spirit are nothing but names of virtues and not the virtues themselves. Unfoldment continues, nourished by the essence attending our soul, while we patiently await His will. Words are merely labels, describing the "fragrance" of those who have arrived at various stages of development. Virtue has many facets. The word "self-reliance" does not possess the power to give courage to those who hear it.

Meditate—and all other values will appear in you as a matter of course. The guidance that brings us out of the realm of fear and trembling results from our decision to live truly rather than to live for ambition and advantage.

Whoever fails for any reason to exercise the life impulse from intuition or understanding serves the link between himself and reality. True self-reliance must come through the illumined consciousness, the inspiration for all our activity. No other goal or concept must lead us. Strength and confidence always develop from exercising understanding, in spite of opposition or encouragement. We must not be moved by any form of religious excitement, nor by the letter of the law—only by a simple illumination each moment. Nor must we seek to know intellectually more than we are capable of doing. Be patient for knowledge. Move as you are inclined, without effort.

If we cannot consciously detach ourselves from our physical body, there is no possibility of control. Until that day of detachment, our consciousness is shackled to the jungle of imagination, just as our thoughts bind us to the inspiration of earthly stimulation through our emotional responses.

Detachment comes about by attachment to a new relativity, between ourselves and the Power that made us. This new relationship is called salvation. It comes by our hungering and thirsting after the right way of life. It is a cry in the dark night of our soul, and the reply to this earnest prayer is a complete shift in viewpoint. We are no longer caught up with our thoughts. Instead, we are sitting back watching them. It is now that we inherit a potential control over mind and body. Without this detached-attached viewpoint, the emotionally-needful soul, easily influenced by stress, is tossed and windswept in the ocean of life. Such a person is related to the stimulation of environment, from which he takes shape by means of his needs and responses.

Seriously considering our pre-ordained purpose, our consciousness becomes detached from the body structure; and at that point of departure, we inherit an understanding by which we can view the nature of the error in ourselves and others. In the light, we groan over what we perceive. We are vexed by our helplessness, yet we can do nothing but be sorry. Our soul, in pain, weeps. And in its travail, it cries to the invisible God to extend compassion.

The reply to the stress of our suffering is control. When we respond to this light, a new pattern of growth, full of hope and life, appears and becomes more evident as the pattern of our error is shattered, step by step.

The consciousness is like a lens between the projected image and the actual reality. We allow invisible fingers of light to shape the play on the screen. The lens is dulled by the emotion we come to need to allow the projection of our own will, design or goals, attended by the dark light of excitement. To allow the flow of life, we must learn to fast from the emotional smorgasbord before us, without retreating from experience.

There is no greater faith than that which is discovered for oneself in the process of unfoldment. The light of understanding will lead you to take decisive action. If you don't know what to do, wait. If you need a reason to act, it can't be right. Right doesn't need a reason—it *is* the reason. As you meditate you will grow to understand true values and the real meanings of words. You will observe that people generally revise their meanings to make their own false ways seem right and your true way, wrong.

To become self-reliant, we must first separate our mind and body from the urgings of a selfish world and see clearly. We must become patient, and when we are truly patient, we are no longer affected by the suggestions of other people, nor directed by them in any way.

Truly, you should not need the approval of others to improve your self-image. When you do a kindness for anyone, let it be done because it is natural to do so, not because you are obligated. Obligation causes secret resentments. If people pressure you with certain obligations, do what is right and reasonable, whether or not it is in line with their suggestion. Do not comply with their impositions simply because you are being pressured. Consider first: is it wise? If it is, do it, not because they want you to do it, but because it is right and wise (in spite of their pressure). Do it because you want to; let them think what they will. As long as you have not acted from obligation, that is all that counts.

A "grace-robber" takes pride in *making* you do what is right, so that he feels like the author of all good and sows confusion in you. But do not rebel at his pressure. This is a negative response which could separate you from reason; that is, you may find yourself not doing what is right (to spite him), or doing the right thing in the wrong way. Even though they seem to be forcing you to do the good thing you would have done anyway, do not resent these people for their indiscretion and grace robbing.

Calmly, without resentment, do what is wise—protest, or

acquiesce. If your employer is pressuring you, explain your inadequacies to him and do the best you can. After that, let him suffer the frustration of any mistakes you might make. (Spilling milk is a mistake, not a sin.)

If people push you to develop too fast, or expect too much from you, don't feel egotistically urged to live up to their expectations or moved to act before you are ready. Move calmly at your own speed, regardless of their ranting and raving, competition, or disappointment in your performance. If they cannot appoint you, they cannot be disappointed in you; if you do not accept appointment, you will never feel the sting of guilt and fear that comes out of such a relationship.

If others encourage you toward what is unwise, tell them politely, "No." Don't respond or give in emotionally to any kind of pressure, regardless of its urgency. You will be aware of the pressure, but keep it from getting under your skin, through patience. Stand calmly upon principle. Bear witness to what you perceive, and you will become stronger each day.

Wait…respond only to what you know is wise…less and less to people and things. Listen respectfully to what people have to say, but allow reason, and not emotion, to dictate your response. Remember also that being for what is right is different from being against what is wrong. Loving right is different from hating wrong and feeling right about it.

Your true compassion is tested, and your unwholesome needs exposed, when you feel threatened or excited by the presence of cruelty or temptation.

Do all things for the love of right, not the fear of consequence or hope of gain, and you will be growing in wisdom and grace.

Don't be too sympathetic. If you are sorry for someone, you become emotionally involved with him and so lose your power to be truly helpful. Be careful how you give to those who try to insult you into being angry and guilty.

A doctor cannot help his patient if he is emotionally involved. Being sorry merely lifts your ego at another's expense, and it causes guilt. Then comes the compulsion to do something to cover that guilt, and this creates more guilt. Then you help too much, making the other person sicker, more dependent, more resentful of your motives.

Be then compassionate, which is caring enough to help in the right way, and only when it is prudent, without the elevation of emotional feeling. Be outspoken about it, with firmness, kindness and patience. In this way, you will be able to help people by not always giving them what they crave from you, and they will come to ask less of you. They will learn to anticipate your wise response and will try first to measure up to their own responsibility before running to you with their problems. Those who are truly worthy will demand little and thereby receive the best gift of all, for they will see and appreciate the light in you.

Your generosity must not function simply as a result of social pressure. And no giving, acts of kindness, accomplishment, or feat of courage must have power to make you feel good. If you feel or react incorrectly, the discrepancy between what you are and what you should be will be revealed to you in secret. You will notice that guilt or fear arises from being excited or taking credit for accomplishment.

Do not be easily obligated to others. Be strong, and say, "I'm sorry"; it is always better to say no than to oblige with reluctance. Also, do not attend anyone's needs because it makes you feel strong or because you feel sorry for him or because he would criticize you if you failed him. Anything you do for these reasons is done only to elevate your wrong self and make it more wrong.

Do all things cheerfully and naturally, without strain or effort, and without worry about the outcome. You must live without effort or strain, without trying. If you have not that strength, wait and meditate for it. Be patient.

Be natural, and speak plainly. Have the audacity simply to be your patient, calm, unexcited self. This is possible when you do not glean your energy from being angry at anyone or anything—even your employment, whether it be "mean" or meaningful. Neither must you desire motivation from the encouragement of others. The virtuous person will not encourage you, other than by his own example; and the person without virtue would not encourage you to goodness, lest he suffer by contrast.

If you are tired, meditate. Be quiet and wait for the strength to do your chores. Do not seek the stimulation of excitement to goad you into activity. Be still and wait for your substance to be renewed from within.

Do not try to manipulate others into doing things for you, with clever words and actions. Everything must be done without thought of what other people will think of you, or what they may do for you in return.

Meditate to serve rightness in all things, and you will be free—free from the bondage of error, to do what is right. Remember, the energy you borrow from the outside to do anything at all will make you untimely, awkward and wrong. Guilty, afraid and dependent upon that excitement, you will be obliged eventually to serve a wrong cause. A state of "reversed being" will exist. You will be addicted to someone or something on the outside, just as you should be dependent upon truth as it is expressed through intuition from the inside.

Just adhere to principle because it is right, regardless of what the outcome will be. Do this, and you will be self-reliant, and you will live unto God.

Watch your relationships with people carefully. Resign from those mutual admiration clubs and from those responses and excitements that elevate and stimulate your pride to feel right. We all know someone who befriends us and gives us sympathy, obliging us to reciprocate. Then, renewed by each other, we go home to the battle front and fight on again in the wrong way. Our need of such friends is an unholy need.

Don't give sympathy. Instead, expose the motives of the person who seeks it!

Meditation will cause you to be more patient and less angry. Soon it will become difficult for you to get excited in the old way—and because you will bear no malice and feel no unholy needs, no one will be able to involve you with intrigue. You will naturally do what is right, regardless of how unpleasant it might be.

The first principle of wisdom is patience. You must overlook because you want to, not because you have to. You must overlook by choice, not by obligation. Being patient is not being upset. Being patient is living without anxiety, in the absence of selfish goals. Being patient is being able to wait; for the good that we receive will come as we abandon our bid for power and glory and our own good self-image.

Patience is the ability to look into the face of hell without resentment, to discern wickedness without being moved emotionally by it.

The meditation exercise allows your higher self to emerge, so that you can deal with life's problems without outside assistance. You will develop a greater trust in the intuition through which the true self makes itself known to the ego. You will have real virtue, and you will be able to enjoy your worldly goods with modesty and without guilt.

174

This exercise is a response to what you know is right. This covers everything. All that follows is a natural unfoldment.

True patience is the foundation of all virtues and gifts. Live each moment honestly, and in that moment you will grow in perception. Quietly say "yes" when you mean yes, and "no" when you mean no.

This dispassionate attitude eliminates guilt and sets you free from the drudgery of easing your conscience with what is more guilt-producing. It eliminates the obligation to live for others, and to call that servitude love.

Some people seem to specialize in drawing you into arguments that you cannot possibly win—anything you say in reply is used against you and exposes you to further criticism. It is often the better part of wisdom simply to agree with such a person and forget about it quickly. We often serve principle best by ignoring the cunning challenge to do battle in its behalf. Remember, "resist not evil."

"If your enemy compels you to go one mile, go with him two." Agreeing with him, without hostility, means here humoring him through good sense, not supplying him with the resistance that would make him feel strong and self-righteous. Overlooking and making allowances must be accomplished with great discretion. This means not being excited or upset, and therefore, not responding, instead of responding inwardly and suppressing outwardly.

If you are doing this exercise correctly, you will not have to make an effort to be patient. You will be secretly amused at what you once thought was serious. Your attention will be to reality, and you will see life without the coloration of emotion. The awareness of your need of patience will accompany you on your journey through each day, like a pleasant strain of music in your soul.

Remember, when you used to become upset, how thoughts would capture your whole attention, and how your negative thoughts would creep back after you had tried to dismiss them? Now that you know patience, you are responding to a different order to life, and your attention will be caught up in reality, away from illusion.

Patience is the greatest and most important of all principles, evidence of the connection to reality. You will discover it gives you the courage and strength to apply other principles as you see them, as each occasion arises. If you are patient, you will be able to rely upon your own good judgment with confidence, weaning yourself away from dependency upon anything or anyone, other than the One who created you in His own likeness.

9

REGENERATION
THE RENEWAL OF THE MIND FROM WITHIN

Meditation is a very simple process—too simple for words.

Meditation *should* be simple, and it should gradually become even more simple. It should never become more complex, or where do you end?

Meditation gives you so little to do that your ego may find it difficult, even unacceptable. Its simplicity is unbearable to an ego that thrives on challenge.

The results, on the other hand, are so profound that we tend to interrupt the process and spoil everything by trying to explain it, take credit for the results, or analyze it and make it work. What we should do as the result of meditation is to observe, wonder and just simply begin to believe the marvelous world of effects taking shape before our very eyes. You see, the less we do (ego-wise), the more good happens. In meditation we see how our ego was involved with everything that went wrong in our lives. Simply recognizing this and doing less ourselves enables good to begin to take shape within us and around us.

Problems fall away by themselves; good things just happen, and everything falls into place without any scheming or planning on our part. It is most humiliating to our pride, which is used to huffing and puffing, making things work only to have them backfire, and giving "good" reasons for everything that ever went wrong in our lives.

In fact, our mind becomes so empty of worry and planning that we have virtually nothing to do, except to understand more, appreciate more, wonder more and see more clearly to avoid problems. As we become more adept at avoiding problems, things become easier, so we worry even less.

Worry has been our substitute for the natural concern we should have had. We just had to worry to ennoble ourselves. It seemed quite normal to worry; but worry is really the compulsive activity of the mind without faith, in the dark, priding itself on solving the problems that worry itself created.

Worry is a counterfeit virtue. Guilty of failing to be creatively concerned, we needed to fill our minds with something, even when we didn't have anything to be concerned about. It did seem the natural thing to do. Could we admit to our failings? Of course not! If we didn't have such busy minds we would be forced to see our faults. So we worried about the war and about the kids. Worry made us industrious busybodies who meddled in every kind of affair for its great pride value. But then we got involved and created problems so enormous that our inability to solve them with worry became apparent—even to ourselves.

Again, worry is the action of a mind in the dark, forgetting the truth, proudly trying to fix what it did in the dark.

We couldn't stop worrying before because we didn't want to stop; it had an ego value for us. It always seemed like love for others. It made us forget our empty, faulty, meaningless existence. It won us badges of honor for this or that cause. Had we a grain of *true concern*, we would never have had anything to worry about—no great activity of mind to testify to our ego's greatness.

Oh! How the vain ego loves to play god and gloat over all the faults of His creation. How little do we realize that we ourselves unconsciously project those problems so that we might be continuously excited over them and be challenged again and again to change them for what seems better (which is in reality much worse) so that once again the spirit of vainglory is challenged to new lows of triumph.

How desperate we have been for others to cry out in need. How we needed their needs, and by "helping," made them need us again. We were glad that no one was perfect, so that we could glorify ourselves by worrying about them and coming to their aid like an angel from heaven.

We once enjoyed taking account of all our grudges and reveling in memories of past glories. This was the substance of our ugly pride. It would sit and worry and reminisce about conquests, and peer into its storehouse of intellectual achievements. Our minds abounded in the knowledge that testified to our glory and *outshouted our growing conscience as it testified to the contrary.*

To all this noise was added the din of distraction that made us forget how wrong we were and made us forget the truth that we labored not for our conscience (which we were wont to disbelieve) but for the spirit of vainglory. We labored for effect; with a few pretty words we tickled other deluded souls to tickle our vanity back again with approval. We infected the world with problems in the guise of love so that we would have something to gripe about, gloat over and worry about—

all of which made us seem to be superior beings.

In exchange for a sense of worth, power and glory, we traded our bodies; we served a wrong purpose, hoping upon hope that the purpose we served would be our very own. With worry we hoped to serve our ego a notion of its concern for others in place of our failure to love them. We focused on the image of ourselves nobly worrying to mask the fact that we were using others to *create* this noble image of ourselves.

What helpless pitiful things we created. Like Dr. Frankenstein, we sired rebellious monsters who soon began to fight against our need to feel saintly, who used our hypocrisies to champion their egos' glory.

In the guise of making them better we made them more imperfect so that we could have a full-time preoccupation of worry to forget our miserable selves.

That must all go. And fall away it will—psychic vampires, wolves in sheep's clothing you will be no more. The deep flaw in your nature is your ego-desire for vainglory, power, love, pleasure, status and importance. You have denied your conscience for a few pieces of silver, and sold your labor and your body for a few lies about your faulty guilty self.

Seeking power and glory, you were in conflict with Reality, whose judgment pierced your illusions as fast as you created them. And now you hate or feel sorry for yourself. You are worried again. Maybe you are in the last stages of worry, fabricating dreamstuff, arguing with yourself, piously seeking intellectual truths as if to agree with your nagging conscience and to make a mockery of its judgment. But then you still feel guilty, for it is the wrong kind of agreement. To *agree* with the truth does not make you right—to become right, *you must live from its urgings!*

"If I were God," you may think secretly, "I could never

forgive me for what I have done, so how could *He* possibly forgive me?" Do you judge the judgment upon yourself in hopes of rising higher than the judgment upon you—much as you do when you anticipate, or "judge," the judgments of other people to get above them? If so, you judge the judgment upon yourself that would not be judgment had you not believed and judged that way in your heart, all because you vainly attributed your shortcomings to your Creator as though no greater justice and mercy than your own existed in this universe.

It is imperative that you have the right intent before practicing meditation. For meditation is a special discipline designed to express the potential pattern of an enlightened reason. When we have found the light that we should consciously and earnestly seek, we must then dramatize it in our lives. Knowing and doing are two separate things that now must be made one. So our motive must be to seek reality first and then to extend that special knowing through the practice of meditation. But not just *any* kind of meditation. The truth must have a truthful way of expressing.

If your motive is not right, you are in danger of becoming locked to or fixated upon the words or the method, and it then becomes hypnosis. If you do not match the proper method to the true knowing, you will block the pathway of expression. When both motive and technology match, you flower and grow; there is no frustration and no fear or worry over the reappearance of old conditions that are played back for correction.

A pure intent awakens us to a new level of awareness that makes available to us a new *power*, containing an information value to remold our minds and redirect our lives from within. Without this truth, emerging through the lens of consciousness to light our way, we tend to become hung up with anything or anyone supposed to help us lift our spirits—including music, religion, positive thinking and mantras.

Although you are able to see more than others in this state, refrain from lording it over them, from making untimely decisions and giving too much advice. Just be. Don't consciously take thought of what to say and when to say it. Let that be spontaneous and natural.

Much of your awakening will occur after meditation, while you are at work or play. Meditation is invariably a painful process because it awakens us to our hidden failings. Eventually the shock of discovery effects a change in our nature. *All* change, good or bad, tends to cause discomfort. Your habits may represent a need to soothe a process of deterioration caused by emotion, namely resentment.

Other excitements, like too much love and affection, designed to help us escape and forget our faults, also cause degeneration and change in unsuspected ways.

Something may try to prevent you from meditating and seek to persuade you that it is unnecessary. Your record player may break. At inconvenient times people intrude, ring the phone and door-bell. Just about everything may happen to prevent you from starting this communion with Reality.

Meditation itself may become boring. It is less and less exciting as we lose the initial contrast of relief. Precisely at the point where you have succeeded in becoming quiet, a flurry of old thoughts, memories (perhaps even commercials), bubbles up for review.

As we live calmly, reacting less to environment, thoughts trapped and supported by emotion, as well as a way of life we developed when we were conditioned to be answerable only to outside pressures, are once again called to mind. This may happen many times. You actually may relive an experience. If you re-dream it during sleep you may play the part formerly required of you.

For example, you may dream out a hostility towards someone. Here you recognize a buried sentiment. Why? Because, while you were not meditating, you were subject to an unseen power that moved you according to its own design, though you believed it to be your will. As you meditate you will observe, by the light of truth, what you once justified, and thus you will become free by a special kind of knowing. The hostilities you once needed to support your ambitions and pride, you assumed to be normal, and therefore you barely noticed them.

New understanding will change your relations in the future with people of the past, and release their hold upon you, even from the grave. You may also dream out a scene where, instead of being angry, you are calm and patient. Thus you will know a change has occurred.

Do not meditate for oblivion. Allow thoughts to appear. Do not dissolve them before they emerge. Such a thing *is* possible. Just watch and observe. Let them come. If your conscious mind wanders off downstream with them, something inside will snap you back to observe them once again and break their hold over you.

Once you can observe a thought without being carried away by it, you will be able to master that thought process. Through steadfast observation, you will destroy the power of each thought in turn.

While it is correct to push aside or dissolve distractions by watching them without anger or fear, do not do this with your bona fide guilts. Observe these and bear the accumulating pain graciously without anger or fear or attempting to deal with them. Soon your past will disappear to the point of forgetfulness. You will begin to feel as though you were just born, made anew.

Babbling trivia and distractions will pour out of your system, alternating with guilts. A level of distraction always conceals a layer of guilt. Step by step, life will lose its stranglehold, its power to turn you on, tempt, uglify and mislead you. Your need for distraction and escape will diminish to the point where you seem not to be interested in anything. Bear this too, for a while. Wait for the wind of the Spirit of truth to provide redirection and motivation.

You may also feel lethargic to the point of appearing to be lazy, not able to do your work. Bear this too, as well as the criticism of others. What you think needs to be accomplished may be a throwback to ancient ties and outgrown obligations; or perhaps the services are appropriate enough, but motivated wrongly; that is, by anger or fear. Just meditate for the strength to do the right thing or to resist the wrong. Upon rising, you will either find the natural strength to accomplish your task or commitment or discover that you have no interest in such obligations, which indicates that they were emotion-based suggestions, entirely motivated by social pressure, having no real value to you or to the motivators.

Often you will experience emptiness. You will feel dull and unqualified as a person, parent or teacher. You will seem to have forgotten everything you know. Wait. Understand this: the Spirit departs for a while to test the inclination of the soul—to see if it will return to its old affiliations.

This meditation is not an affirming process, nor is it a memorizing procedure. To learn it by heart will defeat the objective. It is basically a technology that quietens you, and thereby awakens you to meaning. It induces you to move from that meaning. It gives you back to yourself. For this reason you may dispense with the hand-raising imagery, for that was only an exercise to enable you to control and connect mind, body and soul—to quieten you sufficiently to see meaning. From this point on, *insight* takes the place of imagination.

Images and words are only noises. They can have no real therapeutic effect. At best, they distract you from worry, fear, and pain so that you don't know that you are a problem to yourself and others. The image and noise level in your mind has already replaced your awareness of truth. And without awareness you make mistakes, suffer conscience, and grow to need words and images to argue against reality, as if to offset the deficiency with a fantasia of illusion and concepts.

Verbal suggestions also tend to break a worry cycle that has accelerated your illness. Saturated by suggestions and positive affirmations, you may seem to get better, but unfortunately you might then begin to believe in the therapeutic power of the *word*. What happens in reality is that your illness slows down to a more normal pace, until you become disturbed and accelerate the process again with worry. Words have no power to heal. All they can do is lead you back to your true identity.

There are certain key words which people use to excite you, turn you on and make you feel worthy. Observe how you trap people into saying these words for the turn-on ego-drive value; see also what you trade for them.

Awareness is vital. But there are two kinds of awareness: a self-conscious guilty awareness that doesn't know how to make anything right, makes a mess of everything by trying anyway and then "blanks out" on the problem as a last resort, or the enlightened healthy awareness that is able to come to grips with pressures and keep them outside, and won't let them under the skin.

Your meditation will bring you to this healthy type of awareness, and this always includes a factor of light that shines in the darkness. You may actually see once-invisible forces at work for the first time, and observe them working in you as well as in others.

The imagination is the no-man's-land where evil confers with your vain ego. Here it makes its appeal to your secret wishes. Don't be upset and try to deal with it. You may be somewhat alarmed at the powerful use it makes of the substance or ectoplasm of imagination. It makes you think terrible things to make you believe that *you* are doing all the thinking. It tries thereby to make you feel unworthy of salvation, and seeks an injunction against your meditating so that you will stop. You may be tempted to believe that if you stop you will not see bad thoughts and everything will be all right. For goodness' sake, DON'T STOP MEDITATING!

At every level of growth, that invisible power will be there with a matching temptation. By observing the nature of that temptation, you will see, by its appeal, the nature of your ego and its special weakness. (Repent of this.)

You cannot deal with these forces or "voices" on a psychological level because their origin is not psychological at all. In observing yourself you will occasionally hear vile utterances, antagonistic to reason—just when you think that your motive is sincere. This tends to make you doubt your original intention, tempting you to give up the meditation and observation.

Just understand that *you* are observing a mind that has been controlled and shaped by other forces for a purpose incongruous to its original design. Your physical body and mind, thought stuff, is not the real you; you are the *observer*.

Once your desire is true, you are able to observe what is untrue. What you observe is the old physical self, still under the hypnotic sway of subtle forces that seek to hold you as a slave and make you doubt and despair. Again, those thoughts are *not you*! What *observes* them is the real you. You did not put those thoughts into your mind. If you did, then you could also change them on command. You may once have agreed with, needed, or allowed them. Because your body is still connected to the source of error outside, it is taking shape from the signals it receives from the outside transmitter. It is being used to communicate doubt to your soul, so that you might fear that you can never be right, and so be promoted to give in to sin, to serve your old master well.

But right is observing the wrong. The error that has taken physical shape is using that stolen physical body, as it were. Just keep observing without anger or fear. Don't enter into a dialogue with those thoughts and voices. Just observe until your soul cries out to God.

For the time being, don't call upon a name that you have been educated to accept, or else you may revive a conditioned reflex response to *words* that connect you to the outer world. The savior whom you may have accepted via brainwashing is not the real one. Many of us have accepted a "holy spirit" in a moment of excitement, but it turned out to be the unholy one instead, and by him you justified every sin while you got worse.

These voices may urge you with scriptures for this reason. Of course they are scriptures used incorrectly. The wolves in sheep's clothing posing as ministering angels of God have purposely conditioned you to words and stolen you away from real meaning, life and truth. They have handed you over to error in the *name* of truth.

Such tactics are used to confuse and anger you so that you will be sucked down into despair. Your resentment rekindled against such teachers and memories only makes you feel guilty, makes them look saintly, and involves you with them more than ever.

The voice in your head is the voice of error. Sometimes you may hear two voices, one posing as the good. Disregard them both. Conscience is a silent knowing. The truth rarely speaks to you with words, but is like a light that illumines the darkness and shows you plainly the nature of things. It is a wordless knowing. It goes beyond words and reveals the nature of words.

Thoughts that haunt and nag you can simply be emotions seeking expression, or an emotional catharsis. But there are other factors that you must be prepared to see. You could change your own thoughts, if they were really your own. Grant that there are suggestions in your mind that come from other people, so you will see these as well as their source, as you never have before; but be prepared eventually to see, in the light of your enlightened consciousness, the grotesque thing you have become.

Again, do not react with fear or anger. It may leave your body, contorting your features as it leaves, as it cannot stand upon holy ground. Be aware at all times so that it cannot return. It may use supernatural forces to frighten you: such tricks as moving the bedclothes, sounds of breathing, knocking and the like. Just stay calm. Fear and anger will open the door of your mind again.

Things may seem to get worse for a while. But you will only be seeing what you were hiding from all these years. Your house was burning down but you didn't want to know about it.

We also tend to experience insights and then make the terrible mistake of hanging on to memories of them in order to stimulate the body to recreate those feelings. This is due to an old pattern that you used on yourself to make the past live again. Objects and music, as well as words, have a kind of sentimental turn-on value. Under a spell evoked by words, we can cause the body to re-experience a past excitement; with songs, symbols and beads, we are able to restimulate false religious feelings and behavior to distract us from our failings in the present.

Words and ideas once had power over the body to recreate emotional experiences,"good"or bad. The recall of pleasant memories awakened the body to do the old soft-shoe, causing us to forget unhappiness in the present. For example, think of a lemon and your mouth will water as though you were in the presence of a real lemon.

If you try to hang on to insights like this, you will cut yourself off from the *source* of insight and fall down. Then you will be back in the old rut of clinging to memories again. Don't be afraid to forget. Let your mind learn to be still that you might receive more true experiences and become re-molded and answerable to that new source within.

Children often feel that they are saying or re-experiencing what they have done before. This has given rise to false notions such as reincarnation. When we are young, we are not too far removed from reality—we often see with spiritual eyes things far off, and a pattern of circumstances about to occur. But then our pride swells up—we begin to think we have a great power. Through vanity, then, we become involved with emotional and worldly entanglements, so that we gradually become dull and brutish and lose this great gift.

A vision of things to come may occur, but do not try to

make them work out. Nor must you struggle to interpret their meaning. When this occurs it will simply fit a preordained pattern, so you will know that there *is* a pattern to this drama on earth, and that a mysterious and mighty hand fashions the course of creation according to His secret purpose.

*****

Meditate by just being *aware* of yourself.
Watch your thoughts.
Be aware of your feelings.
Observe yourself.
You may become aware of light patterns…superimpose them over any distracting thought—to be *aware*.
Let that awareness then be directed into your hand as it becomes a pulsation of energy.
It will feel as though the blood is flowing down into it. Thus awareness shall grow as a living force from within, stronger than outside pressures.
Let thoughts come out of hiding. Don't be carried away with them. If your mind wanders off, become *aware* again.
Observe those thoughts.
Look through the middle of your forehead.
Feel the fingers tingling.
Awareness becomes more aware.
Insight grows to see errors.
Be *aware* of them with the light of new knowledge.
Your presence of mind becomes a Presence in mind and body for good, so you are less affected by the negative pressures and principalities.
Don't resent what comes to light. Bear the pain of failings.

Don't blame anyone. Be *aware* of your part of the past or present trouble or involvements.

Seeing the compulsiveness of your own behavior and attitude, you might then have some compassion upon those who mistreated you in the past.

Observe pains, tensions, emotions and thoughts. They are trying to tell you something. Each tells a story. Each represents a wrong way in which you reacted to life and people and things.

Don't try to change what you see.

Just be aware of what calls upon your attention to observe it.

Don't escape from the facts before you, inside or out.

Bear the discomfort graciously without anger or fear.

Don't expect anything, or else you will make impossible the protocol of grace.

If you have no results and you are angry, realize your wrong motive and proud ego-game-playing.

Understand that, of yourself, you can do nothing. You cannot even make a decision to be right and fair. You can only desire, yearn, hunger and thirst after righteousness continuously—and yearn for the privilege of being able to make a right choice and to be free from error.

Do not be so proud as to think that you can free yourself from the clutches of error and temptation. And when you are able to choose, it will not be by your own powers, but through the strength of grace by which you are again given the power to live correctly and to rule in your body. For this be thankful. And until then, be patient.

Regardless of how pure your motives may be now, they have not always been so.

We all have been tested and our secret ambitious nature was revealed choice by choice, mistake by mistake—and covered, excuse by excuse.

A proud, judging, self-justifying nature it has been, loving only to be exalted in return. Hope that you will come to see this, as well as your servitude to pressures and temptation, which you erroneously called "loving devotion."

This dreaming, ambitious, goal-seeking, selfish, now tortured and lustful nature, must be sorry and must petition for a last chance to make right and fair decisions.

Thinking yourself worthy, you are unworthy. Seeing your unworthiness, you may become worthy of grace. If you think yourself worthy, you will expect a reward, and you will receive only frustration for your vanity.

Moment by moment from that point of grace (of which you cannot be proud) you will see reality more clearly and begin to live more effortlessly, in accordance with intuitive urges, without scheming and planning as before. Always new layers of faults will be unpeeling, accompanied first by remorse and then change.

The pain is less each time, but the problems are more subtle.

Be *aware* at all times.

Do not let yourself be caught up with worldly affairs so that you lose sight of what is going on, inside or outside.

Do not be hung up with these words, this lesson, or anyone or anything.

Do not study intellectually, as though the sheer weight of information could make you better.

See the meaning of words.

Do not force understanding.

Wish you could understand…and wait.

The words and experience shall become a key to awaken you to meaning, in time. Meaning then will give you new direction, causing false beliefs to be changed.

True ideals, once accepted mechanically by rote, will now take on meaning. Your new development is answerable to the power of God that is making you new.

Before, your "buttons" were pressed by outside forces; the stimulations that excited you caused memories and patterns of behavior that were answerable to and set in motion by the words, signals, impressions, people and things that originated them.

Do not struggle to remember. It will be a case of not being able to forget the good, which will become part of your being, and not being able to remember the bad—only the good lesson derived from the bad experience.

Never cling to old experiences or new revelations.

Just keep being *aware*, clearing your mind by observing and repenting, stressing the Spirit of truth to extend compassion.

Be still, and know in a new way.

Do not depend upon memories (no matter how meaningful they were) to decide your next action or word. Wait. Know that you do not know.

Soon you will have an answer.

Be patient, calm. Quieten your racing mind, which worries unnaturally and reaches for wrong answers.

Thus you may feel the discomfort of outer problems, but they will not disturb you and get under your skin.

Resist the tendency to doubt, and more wisdom will come to bring you far beyond your present limitations.

Let the light of each revelation that shapes you, in thought, word and deed, collate the past information of word, thought and deed to deal with the ever-present. But for you it will be effortless and easy—as though a light were shining on your path.

You will gasp (as an observer) in wonder, and become renewed in faith. Observe without excitement, and what is truly valuable will simply stay with you.

Don't decide what is right by analysis.

Just observe.

Be aware.

Discern. Don't judge. When you get rid of the anger and the excitement, your judgment will become a healthy discerning, and from this impartial viewpoint you can act and speak.

Give up suspicion as a defense. You become suspicious only when you trust without seeing clearly in the light. You become too trusting only when you lose faith in your own judgment and are forced to depend upon others, who are either blind or malicious.

Accept and reject calmly.

Do not force yourself to learn.

Just observe.

Remember what you will, whatever interests without excitement.

Let your desire for seeing reality, living truly and living the meaning for which you were made take first place to everything.

Don't let your mind be cluttered with worldly worries or thoughts of gain, love, power and glory. Those things will come as a matter of course.

Let your emphasis be on desiring to see truly, being fair and honest with others. Then, out of this, all of your talents and business will develop in due course.

Deal with firmness, kindness and patience.

Overlook offense, which means: look the fault and motive of anyone straight in the eye without being angry or upset. Discern, perhaps sternly. Don't judge. You are judging when you are angry.

See that your hostility over the failings of others is an unhealthy ego-need to look superior or right compared with them.

Anger and secret resentment excite you and make you unable to see exactly what is wrong with you, while you become too engrossed in what is wrong with others.

As you calm down and give up judgment, you will see your faults come to light.

Observe.

Be patient with your own self. Be patient with others.

See how easy it is to be patient with yourself then.

Don't judge. Don't be angry or sorry for yourself. That was the old ego way of being better than your conscience.

Desire only to be able to live differently.

For persistent problems, feel the pain of not being able to choose rightly until it grows to become true repentance, which, being acceptable to God, will enable Him to extend compassion, which for you is your *discovery of being able to make a right choice*, which is true gratefulness leading to a procession of joys.

As you grow, you will uncover layers of faults which are preceded by a flurry of meaningless thoughts, causing some pain as before. Just keep observing and being sorry.

Soon they too will change.

Do not be excited to anger.

Discern, don't judge.

See the fault, yes. Stare hell straight in the face without flinching or becoming upset. Don't become frightened or feel compelled to exceed or overcome, excel or defeat. Stay calm.

Neither must you be uplifted as holy men by praise, but overlook praise graciously.

Meet life, people and things calmly, with dignity and

without pretense.

Nothing must lift your spirits.

Be yourself.

Do not derive a feeling from your children, friends, spouse or animals.

The trying of your understanding produces patience, so that you are calm and unruffled in the face of torment and cruelty, no matter how petty or gross.

Through patience you will come to perfection.

It is ambition that sets us apart from the purpose for which we were created and makes us impatient and imperfect. We may not see this as long as we succeed in getting what we want, and obtaining "love" from creatures and people.

When your consciousness desires its true meaning and purpose again, and nothing is more important, suddenly your anxiety is gone. You will have discovered patience with people and things.

PART 2

HEALING
AT THE CAUSE

10

Can Guided Imagery Cure Disease?

For forty years I have been hearing the same old line that cancer patients can think themselves to a stronger immune system using relaxation and guided imagery techniques. The latest scientist to make this pronouncement as if it were a brand new discovery is Professor Leslie Walker, Director of the Institute of Rehabilitation and Pharmacology Health at the University of Hull in northern England. Guided imagery, she says, can also help patients to cope more effectively with the disease.

This study, which was funded by the Cancer Research Campaign charity, made it clear that while such techniques did indeed boost immune cells, the effect upon the disease itself is not well known. The report went on to say that there was no proof that psychological interventions could prolong survival. When researchers tested all of the 80 women involved with a test group, they found that those who successfully practiced the relaxation techniques had higher numbers of important immune systems cells. The net result was to demonstrate that in some mysterious way even patients with large tumors receiving immunosuppressive treatment, such as chemotherapy, surgery, and radiotherapy, could indeed produce some measure of immunological change. Apparently, they have not successfully cured anyone to date. The only possible reason for this is that the scientific community has failed to understand the underlying principle of disease.

Fully 80 percent of all illnesses—mental, emotional, and physical—are believed to be emotion-based, including some forms of cancer. Science is certainly on to something, but they are missing a piece of the puzzle that they can never find, simply because the answer lies beyond psychology.

The problem with contemporary psychology is that it is godless, and for this reason alone it will never find the key to solving the mystery of any of the emotion-based problems. Most psychologists and researchers have the notion that the brain of man reigns supreme, and that the intellect has some kind of god-like power to heal. Experiments indeed do show that as a man thinks, to some degree his physiology is so ordered. Even so, suppose that it were possible to use positive thinking or guided imagery, imagining bad cells being overcome by the good ones. You would have to spend most of your life preoccupied with imagery, leaving little time for details.

Not having found the source of negative thoughts, emotions would eat away at all of your positive efforts. There is no doubt that thought can influence health and behavior. The problem is: how do we keep positive thoughts from having to struggle against an influx of negative ones? From whence negative thoughts? If you are the source of your thinking, why aren't you in control naturally, and if you are not, then who is? The answer is simple. One need only understand the dynamic.

There are three components of your identity: your body, your brain, and your spirit, which is your consciousness or your soul. You are not your body; neither are you your thoughts, but if you are fused to your emotional thinking, that is the reason you have lost control and why you are in such trouble.

The reason you are lost in your thoughts and fused to your emotions is denial. Emotions sustain a reality that is different from what Reality requires of you. You're not supposed to be lost in your thinking like Alice in Wonderland. You need to be objective, the observer of thought. Only from the place of observation, not entangled with thought stuff, can you exert effortless control. The problem with all of us is that as we go through life, we get more and more lost in a maze of thoughts, seeking answers in our intellect. Down there in the darkened theater of our mind, we seek also to escape into fantasy from the pain of reality.

So do you see that in order to have real life, you need to be the watcher? As the watcher, the observer of thoughts, you can begin to realize that the watcher is also being observed: you experience this as conscience. It is a spiritual thing. You may be the captain of the ship but not the builder or the owner. Realizing this, you may see the need to take your orders intuitively. If you will find your way to fulfill this purpose that is other than your own, you will experience something known as oneness with God, and thus you will inherit a natural ascendancy over your mind and body. Christians call this experience "salvation."

The problem you now face is that, in a manner of speaking, your ship is controlling you and as the captain you have lost contact with the owner. You have betrayed the trust of your maker. The spirit of betrayal guides you toward the rocks. You are lost, without a meaningful goal or destination, immersed in the struggle to solve your problems, tossed helplessly by the wind. None of your own solutions or goals has any meaning. All Captains need a given destination and purpose.

You need to see what the problem is: the observer has become hopelessly tangled up with thought. Your conscience pursues you. That entire willful struggle against the tide of emotions and imagination is futile and does nothing but distract you from your real purpose in life, whatever that is. You alone should be in charge of your emotions; but in your selfishness you have given power to others in exchange for their support.

You need now to find salvation from all those friendly betrayers. You cannot bring good into the world nor do what you know is right in your heart as long as you slavishly respond to what is wrong. Your response to pressure signifies obedience to the wrong One World order.

Uncontrollable thoughts flow up from your emotions, sustained by the wrong way you react to people, places, and things. Such emotion is evidence of a mystical failure of your consciousness to reject seductive pressures and temptations that your ego needs to survive. Your over-sensitivity allows thoughts to flow from the pressure root. As I have said, such thoughts are negative only because emotions, triggered by guilt obligations and intimidation, reverse the flow of how life was designed to be. Overreaction triggers emotion, which translates the will of others into negative thoughts rushing into your head. Your consciousness is pulled down into a whirlpool of thinking and there remains imprisoned. Slowly but surely, you begin to live in a virtual thought world of reality, emotionally sustained by compulsive reactions, obsessed by feelings of hate and revenge. In religious parlance, that experience is known as judgment.

202

All emotions that arise from excitement disconnect you from your own control and allow penetration by the ill will of tormentors. Something in people compels them to enslave you to what has enslaved them. To state it simply, your own spiritual weakness, sustained by the excitements of resentment and anger, has separated you from Divine Love and is slowly but surely transforming you into a hate-love slave of hate-love objects.

Various sensual pleasures related to rage are always transferring your soul's allegiance to the teases of intimidators. Resentment will always be the handmaiden of judgment that, in turn, translates into all those unhealthy sensual responses to the intimidator and therefore results in a form of slavery to new owners. In a manner of speaking, you're being boarded and taken over. Emotion plants an alien identity within you that becomes the basis of many kinds of illnesses—mental, emotional, and physical—including certain kinds of malignancy. Ultimately this identity grows to think of itself as "you" and appropriates your immune system unto itself. Surely this explains autoimmune diseases. The body attacks itself because it senses a transfer of power to a different entity.

Using a different analogy, your conscience is the Sentry at the Temple door. If the watcher sleeps, then the Temple can be taken by storm, ravaged and corrupted by another life form which slowly but surely, upset by upset, resentment upon resentment, begins to take shape inside you as though it were you. "Its" thoughts become your thoughts. It thinks through you and eventually becomes you so that you don't really know who you are anymore.

Do you see now how your illnesses are more spiritual than pathological: disease is the symptom, the manifestation of a spiritual cause. If, as the good book says, your body is the Temple of the living God and the spirit dwells within it, then your soul is the guardian with a certain responsibility and allegiance. Your road to recovery should be to discover what this responsibility is so as to be restored to favor in the sight of Him who created you. Unless you are ready to delve deeply and sincerely into this mystery, you may never be well. Medicine and drugs for all diseases have value, but one must be very wise in their use. Never use them as though they were the ultimate cure. Use common sense to continue to seek the actual cause in your nature, and watch your responses.

Pride, sustained by tainted emotions, is the root cause of 80 percent of all illnesses, mental, emotional, and physical, not to mention problems with marriage, children, and business. Resentment forms and nurtures the alien in our being. Puffed up with pride's emotional essence, your soul is tainted and cut off from the eternal living force within you. Pride, sitting there unholy on the throne of the holy, becomes addicted to the feelings that have always provided you with a sense of worth. It lives in you through being sustained by the very same emotions the parent spirit used to penetrate you traumatically in the very beginning. The emotional addiction you equate with being alive is the illusory life that leads to death in the service of an insidious purpose other than that for which you have been created.

In order to solve any problem, you must know its root cause. Perhaps you need a little more explanation in order to grasp the seriousness of the problem that you are facing. It is quite possible that your new understanding, painful though it may be, has already grasped the meaning of all this; if so, you might experience a quick healing. It might be advisable to stop reading at this point and just let it happen. Refrain from memorizing this text. These words are meant only to awaken you from your intellectual dream state and shock you into a sense of awareness as to what your problem really is. This awakening can be somewhat upsetting and painful. Nevertheless, bear the pain with humility, minus the usual resentment of the source of your knowing. Suffering the pain of conscience, without running from it into emotion and thought stuff, will allow the friction of God to humble and heal you in your relationship with Him.

Emotion does more than stain the soul with pride; it draws you away from the Eternal Source of love, life, and understanding. Emotion has submerged your soul into a semi dream world of virtual reality, a reality emotionally shaped and sustained. Emotion clouds clarity and alters perception so that we see friends as enemies and enemies as friends.

If you have been violated by injustice, you have probably adulterated your natural clarity of discernment by reacting with judgment of the source. Here you find yourself in conflict with God's purpose and incurring His judgment upon your secret judgment of others. Unfortunately, the spirit of pride will not let you admit to guilt. It urges you to seek the emotional salvation known as "emotional security." Usually, the very kind of emotion that introduced the nature of pride draws you toward the kindred spirit in your comforters. Ego, being always threatened in the light of its own faults, is driven to deny its own wrongs by judging the wrongs of others. That way you try to stay ahead of the judgment upon you by making people fail, misinterpreting what they say and do, and secretly judging them for those mistakes. Unfortunately the judging never works. Not only does it fail to relieve the pain; it intensifies conflict with everyone including you.

And so you again seek refuge from this judgment through more and more emotion.

Emotional security turns out to be nothing but denial through the misuse of friends. Even good friends cannot save you; all they can do is save you from salvation with the sympathy of their worldly love. And so it comes to pass that it takes more and more emotion to save you from more and more guilt. The reason the guilt increases is that the saving is wrong, consisting merely of a feeling of being right.

This kind of reassurance is bound to fail and, turning into hate and blame, it produces guilt again and again. The best that so-called compassionate love can do is to encourage you to be more angry, selfish, and unforgiving. Such love inflames hate toward everyone, including those friendly saviors, and never cures anything. Perhaps you can now see what internalized rage does to your immune system. Surely you would be better off learning to be more patient under stress and thus endure injustice with a little more character and dignity. Herein lies the secret of the perfect life; deal perfectly with imperfect people.

Forgive and you will be forgiven.

11

Confronting the Enemy

Just recently it was my sad duty to bury a friend. This emotional moment at the graveside was a valuable teaching tool to drive home an important philosophical point to the grieving congregation. The message I gave them was not for the dead but for the living, to illustrate the true purpose of life. The most important moment of our lives, I said, is the day we die, because it represents the sum total of what we have made of ourselves in our journey through life.

All of us have a person within a person, an identity that develops according to the way we respond to life. All living creatures are shaped in obedience to changing circumstance. They are solely creatures of environment. On the other hand, humans are not; we have choices to conceive a right or a wrong, good or evil. Depending upon the inclination of the soul, the self will unfold from the chosen source.

If you are able to stand without fail for what is right, to hold fast to the truth of every moment with dignity and grace under pressure, if you never yield to seductive appeals but patiently endure, something wonderful begins to happen. A bright nature appears inside you and grows to maturity within your mortal frame. This nature takes a whole lifetime to grow, and eventually becomes the self we know as character. Character embodies the true nature of the loving God. Character is the eternal self that survives the death of the body. Survival of the fittest is the law of nature. Survival of the most noble emerges from the spiritual law.

Our bodies are a mortal bridge spanning the chasm between two dimensions. And when death comes, as indeed it will, we will be drawn to the spirit that guided us through life. Your journey is like the path across that bridge. When the bridge of the body collapses, a force awaits your coming through time.

THE MEANING

Life is not merely eating, drinking, being merry, grabbing all the gusto you can get. You must know by now that life is much more than that. Something is required of us. Material things are good, and it is also good that we should enjoy them. We should enjoy our loved ones too, but not too much. Be careful not to make people, places, and things more important than what is right. Become too attached, too emotionally involved, and you will surely bring about those moments of truth that require soul-wrenching decisions.

Yes, we must love others, but not so much as to desert our principles and core values. They say you cannot eat principles; yet principles constitute a food that sensual man knows nothing about.

208

Commitment to a right source involves everyone in a secret war. In religious parlance, it is the private war between faith and doubt, seeking the love of God or love from the world. If you exchange the security from your family for a compromise on principle, you will earn nothing but contempt. Never would you be worthy of anyone's respect, no matter how much you grub in the dirt for it. All things are wholesome until that moment of truth comes: the gravitational pull between two kinds of loving commitment, the question being whether you are being controlled, manipulated through your affections and material possessions. If so, you are building a house on sand.

Once the gauntlet has been thrown down and the manipulative selfishness of friends and loved ones is revealed comes that moment of truth. Whatever you do, resist the temptation to be angry and upset. Because resentment, as I have explained many times, tends to make you feel guilty as though you have done something wrong, when it is those you resent who are guilty.

Hostility separates you from your own good and makes you feel insecure. Resentment is the key word here. Resentment, anger, hurt feelings, rage, jealousy, being annoyed, aggravated, frustrated, are all different words for one and the same thing: hatred. And hatred separates you from divine love and makes you feel unloved and insecure. The net result is that you find yourself seeking love from the very people that need correcting. So, by giving in and surrendering for a little reassurance, you are empowering the kind of behavior that will eventually hurt you more. Now do you understand why you have to stand up and not be too worried about whether anyone loves you or not? It is your true loving (in this case, your correction) that carries the day and changes the course of everyone's life.

You have many such moments of truth, and in times to come, there will be many opportunities to change sides. Take notice that when you stand firm on principle, revealing your allegiance to what is right rather than your former slavish devotions, mark you well, you may find yourself alone. Therefore, weigh carefully your decision concerning this path through life. Once you stand up, you must never go back to giving in, except, of course, when others are right and you are wrong, because that is the right thing to do. There is an old saying, "A coward dies a thousand times before his death; the valiant die but once."

To enjoy the good life, as indeed you should, you must be its master, not its slave. To possess anyone or anything is to be possessed through everyone and everything, and become ever more insecure. Possessions, achievements, are merely compensations for that something missing, the hollow in your soul.

More often than not, what appears as love is a wolf in sheep's clothing. Cruelty hides behind the mask of hypocrisy, love, and friendship. When it is confident that you have become sufficiently dependent on its affection, off comes the mask.

TWO SIDES OF MATTER

Good and evil live on opposite sides of matter. Let me address the positive side of matter first, the one from which creation came. As I write these words, I can see my thoughts flit across my mind. It is as though I'm sitting in a movie theater absorbed with the play. If I become too involved, I forget that I am in my seat. For a little while, I forget who I am because I have identified with the actors, the images on the screen. The analogy to what is going on in my head is perfect because in the same way, if I'm not careful, I will forget who I am and become someone else.

The point I am making is that we all have that side of consciousness wherein resides the guiding light, from which we are to unfold in a heavenly order, so to speak. As the Lord's Prayer says, "Thy will be done on earth as it is in heaven." Absorbed into your emotionally sustained thinking, you will draw just the opposite your way. By surrendering through anger and need, you enslave yourself to the wrong kind of love and fulfillment. Damned if you get love; damned if you don't.

When the truth dawns, that reality, if it is welcome (and painful though it may be), will save you from the agony of choosing right from wrong. Because the light makes His will known, your path becomes clear, and because your allegiance is to the light, the way is obvious. To you it will be the right thing to do, but most likely not to everyone else, because where you are coming from may be a threat to the selfish willfulness of others.

There is no real courage or virtue without such willful temptation. The moment you choose the right way, things will never be the same and neither will you. Reveal your true self, and people will reveal their true selves, and the battle lines are drawn. So it will be for the rest of your life until the day you die.

You experience the dark side of the force when, through insecurity, you get into people, places and things. When you get into something you can see, something you cannot see gets inside you. In this way, evil projects exponentially to control the whole world. Henceforth your love for others will come from being into God's love and God's love being into you. You will be evolving in accordance with your Creator's will, incorporating His identity into yours, forever growing in Him and He in you. You will be able to love people without needing them, possibly even to reveal to them the true self and the love they have left behind to become what they are.

What they may reject in you is that same truth they have rejected in themselves, yet through this experience with you, real friends and family will emerge. Everyone will try you, but some will come to love you as they should. You can save your family only through being saved from the need of their love, having in that place the need for God's love, revealing it through patient endurance, graciously giving what is good, and resisting what is not. Yours will be the strength good people respect and predators fear.

Surely you can see how vulnerable your loved ones are? They are too immature to realize why they deny what to you is simple common sense. You must help save them from the love of the world while risking their love for you. Giving into their nagging and demanding, for fear of losing their affection, will involve you as the extension of their world.

Confronting your own private hell is the first order of business. And the moment you elect to do so, a big weight will fall away from your shoulders, and you will be carefree, immune, and inoculated against the wickedness of the world, and what is more evident, free from most diseases and sufferings that plague the rest of humanity.

WINNING IS SIMPLY NOT LOSING

Remember those two places where the adversary exists. The adversary projects through environment, through people.

And through traumatic events it lives on through you.

The medical profession acknowledges that about 80 percent of most disorders, mental, emotional, and physical, are due to stress. Stress is indeed our problem. However, the stress humans encounter that causes illness and mental breakdown is not the kind experienced by animals. We are dealing here with something malevolent and spiritual.

The good book tells us that the weapons of our warfare are not carnal, but mighty enough, through God, to pull down strongholds: to cast down imaginations and every high thing that exalts itself against the knowledge of God, and to bring into captivity every thought counter to the obedience of Christ. For animals, there is a merciless natural adversary for the survival of the fittest body.

For mankind, the survival of the fittest is the survival of the noblest spirit. Our merciless adversary is of a spiritual dimension, operating through the realm of materiality and the flesh. The struggle is between the forces of good and evil, and our bodies are the chess pieces in the drama of life and death that is the trying of our souls.

The evidence of wrong allegiance is in the way you respond to pressure. Your body cannot stop reacting because it will not obey you; it is not subject to you because you are not yet subject to God. You have yet to make your commitment. When your will becomes His Will, only then will you have the natural governance over your mind and body to effortlessly overcome your adversary's willfulness. Your sensitivity to the world begins to decrease in proportion to your patient forgiveness. Heretofore, your emotional thinking has fused your consciousness to the flesh and made you a prisoner of your imagination. As long as you live in denial, you will be the prisoner of an emotionally sustained virtual reality.

The guilt that trails you holds the potential unfolding of what you might have been and what you can now be. Your conscience has not condemned you as you have thought; instead it desires to save you. For salvation to occur, you must repent and you cannot know repentance until you move towards the anxiety, instead of running from it into your imagination, as has been your custom.

You must be willing to stand still and let the Divine Presence catch up with you and increase your anxiety. Hold your ground as the pain of conflict increases to a point where you surrender to the inner pressure, in much the same way you have done with outer pressures when the heat was on. Resist the temptation to run away into pleasure and confusion. The problem is that you have identified with the adversary nature that has made a home in you. Understanding all this will enable you to separate from the taint of the ego self.

The only self you have ever known is this false self, which thinks itself to be you, while you have thought yourself to be it. It thinks through you, and you think that is your thinking and feeling.

When you see that your thoughts are not your thoughts, you will also realize that you really have never known who you really are. What remains standing in the light is the little child crying for the father it has never known.

When the memory of the things that you have done in your life is once again called to mind, you will realize with great relief, that it is not you that has felt condemned all along, but the nature that made a home in you. You will no longer feel hostile to God, to your dad, your mother, or anyone. You will feel forgiven and relieved of resentment and judgment upon others, and for this reason all your symptoms and unhappiness will go away. Future stress will continue to be the stresses of injustice and betrayal, but you will be delighted to find yourself dealing with them in a new and masterful way.

OF YOURSELF YOU CAN DO NOTHING

Remember that the first stress is within. There is no longer any need to struggle with your compulsions. Struggle, as you have experienced it, arose from acts of a faithless will that only compound the problems. Your struggle with internal problems has the same consequence as the struggle with people, which is to say you energize and empower them.

Forgiving is the same as right standing with God, which translates into forgiving yourself. In other words, to forgive is the same as being able to forgive yourself. Struggling with the symptoms of emotionally transmitted illness also compounds your problem. Being upset with your symptoms simply empowers the disease.

I have said that some forms of cancer are caused by another identity emotionally introduced, appropriating the immune system to itself. The body's cells are helpless against the intruder, and the soul has lost the sovereignty of its natural power to govern the body.

Unless this condition is thoroughly understood, doctors have little choice but to do what they do best to help the patient survive. So they employ chemotherapy to kill the immune system because it works against the person. Most likely it's not so much the chemotherapy that does the trick, but more so the suffering and torture of the treatment itself which brings patients to their senses, back to reality and humility. The spirit of cruelty takes pleasure in your defeat; it wants you to be upset, resentful, hateful and judgmental. It wants you to puff up with pride and egotistically struggle in the battle of the wills knowing it will have you in the end. So it seems that the only way to win is not to play the game. Let go and let God.

12

Waking Up on the Inside

HELPING THE DOCTOR CURE YOU

What an embarrassment it was to wake up one morning and find myself deathly ill from some unknown malady. It was embarrassing because I have been in the public eye for forty years on the radio. I've written many books on the subject of emotional health. So you see my dilemma; my audience must have rolled up their eyes in disbelief at a man who teaches others to stay well only to get sick himself.

I became sicker and sicker, developing just about every recognizable sickness. I haven't had a pain-free moment in twenty years, but there are no regrets. Naturally I'd rather it didn't happen, but since it did, I practiced what I have preached and used the stress of suffering, as well as the humiliation of the mockers and scoffers, to make me a better man and strengthen my character. The bonus was that what I understood in theory deepened through experience. Knowledge must serve to bring you to its fulfillment, which is enlightenment. Knowledge then acts as a vehicle complementing that understanding. However, the true power of healing lies not so much in knowledge, but in what it brings you to: understanding. That alone contains the life force for change.

I've always preached that well-meaning doctors as a whole do not properly understand their own medical science. While skillful surgeons have twice saved my life (for which I am very grateful), had the 20 or so doctors who treated me understood not only the simple cause, but also all symptoms that evolved from it, I wouldn't have needed those marvelous surgical skills. As the good book says, "Everything bad happens for good to those who love the Lord." I happen to be one of those who believe that with all my heart.

Therefore, I'm writing this in the hope of guiding you through your personal hell, or as the case may be, to give you the missing part of medicine so you do not have to end up as I did. The secret has to do with having the best of both worlds, the spiritual and the practical. Therefore let me give you a word of caution: do not put all your faith in medicine.

I would venture to guess that probably half of the knowledge medical students learn at school is right, while the other half is wrong, and most don't know which is which. The emphasis in school is that diseases are pathological by nature and the emotional-nutritional-spiritual factor is all but ignored. So many are graduated from medical college dumbed down, with little or no intuitive diagnostic sense, with too much reliance on pharmaceuticals, antibiotics and other drugs.

Many diseases have a lot to do with what might be called lifestyle "choices," the basis of which is some kind of rebellion against injustice. While you have the freedom to choose a lifestyle, those choices are invariably emotionally

218

driven, and for that reason they are wrong. The pain of a life wrongly lived leads to conflict, which in turn leads to the comfort factor, which can be anything from religion to drugs, alcohol and doctors. Most people have become so secure in their comfort zone with their enablers that they literally die from the cure.

PEOPLE DEVOLVE; TECHNOLOGY EVOLVES

Chemistry has given people a longer lifespan, which permits them to live longer only to become more wrong, and hence need new medicines to deal with those "new diseases." Evolving diseases require more research, sophisticated medicine and antibiotics. As behaviors are excused by medicine, people devolve and technology evolves. The net result is a demoralized society, kept alive by an enabling science that creates more complicated diseases and value-neutral people. Sooner or later drugs and antibiotics fail. Bugs become stronger; people become physically weaker, spiritually retarded, empty and malevolent; all this leads to chaos and social upheaval. When law, religion and medicine justify or otherwise remove the consequences for behavior, terrible things happen. Penicillin cured syphilis and gonorrhea and saved many lives. Alas, instead of being a blessing, medicine became a curse. Freed from the consequences of the scourge of those diseases, people were emboldened to live more promiscuously, which led to the epidemic of incurable AIDS. Not only can we not cure AIDS as it decimates whole populations, now antibiotic-resistant syphilis and gonorrhea are back to haunt us with a vengeance.

Even more bizarre, when medical science could not diagnose and cure homosexuality, doctors and scientists excused their failure and made it normal behavior. People dying from AIDS are now considered heroes. As lawlessness begins to reign, more scoundrels will be bred than decent people, and we begin to see lawlessness lawfully excused. In other words, the collective egos of establishments, governments, medicine and religion all tend to act very much the way individuals do when they will not face their failures; they adapt to them, excuse them, make wrongs right and make the problem go away. The unwashed masses will elect a despot who will tear down the Constitution, make lawlessness law; insanity and ill health will become accepted as normal, and truth will be outlawed. Indeed, just look around and you'll see it is already happening.

Having learned much from experience not in books, I hope I do not contradict myself by writing one. I desire only to be instrumental in raising your consciousness to such an objective state that you will be able to intuitively see all you need to know for yourself. Your circumstances and situation may be different, but your Inner Light will show you the path.

UNCOMMON SENSE

Very few people are able to recognize a rough diamond lying on the beach the way I would. You see, I was once a journeyman diamond cutter by profession, so I know a diamond when I see one. In much the same way, we all have a hidden wealth of untapped intuitive knowing that has nothing to do with any learning or experience. In religious parlance, that lifestyle is called "living by faith and walking in the light." To say that we have forgotten this intuitive knowing would not be quite correct; that we can rediscover it would be closer to the truth. So, if you will divest yourself of ego and truly search for an answer, with a true desire to know and understand, you will be given to know it when you see it; the answer will almost leap out at you. If something is wrong, it will not sit well; if it is right, it will be self-evident. The way will always be clear and it will seem as though there is no other choice but the way before you.

Allow me to tell you a story to illustrate the point. A young soldier was walking around the parade ground picking up pieces of paper, throwing them down, muttering to himself, "That's not it." He did this for months on end. So his sergeant, being tired of all this, sent him to the shrink. As the soldier continued muttering to himself, the psychiatrist examined him. Finally the doctor concluded his analysis and gave him his discharge papers. And with that, he stopped picking up those pieces of paper muttering, "That's not it." and with a shout of delight, exclaimed, "That's it!" You see, he knew it when he saw it.

The Supreme Court judge was once asked how he defined obscenity from art, and he said, "I know it when I see it." I sincerely hope that this writing helps you know it when you see it in your time of trouble.

THE MISSING LINK

My renowned medical radio doctor friend, Donald Corrow, told me that I had the missing half he needed. It has become far too easy to prescribe a pill for everything as if the symptom were always the cause. There is no doubt that a symptom can also be the cause, but more often than not that is not the case, as with psychosomatic illness. My story begins with an original physical origin of the dozens of causes and effects that almost killed me.

Even seasoned physicians know that it is not always easy to recognize diseases by their symptoms. Different diseases often produce identical symptoms with subtle variations apparent only to a trained observer. A disease can have a psychosomatic basis as well as a physical cause, so that your doctor might treat the obvious and wonder why you do not improve. This is why it is so important to have all your ducks in a row. You will be a much easier patient for any doctor to help if you are spiritually, psychologically and emotionally centered. Then, if the problem does not go away, you will be given to see more clearly into the physical bases of the problem. Your doctor's treatment will become a blessing to you instead of an addiction.

LIFTING THE VEIL

My journey to well-being lasted twenty years from the day I became ill. Fortunately for me, solving the problem was not complicated by emotional factors, for which reason I was eventually able to see clearly right to the original cause. Unfortunately I suffered terribly for about four years before stumbling upon the first clue to my illness.

Having been healthy for the first fifty years of my life, I had no understanding of anatomy. I didn't know quite what a pancreas was, and don't laugh—I didn't even know that I had a prostate. Only when I suddenly became ill, and ran in futility from doctor to doctor, did I look under the hood in order to help myself. At that point, I needed the medical and anatomical instruction manual.

Most people have little interest in the subject of cancer until they become afflicted. So when the doctor diagnosed me with prostate cancer, I knew I wasn't that type. I knew that the doctor was dead wrong and the biopsy confirmed it. Believe it or not, as all the other symptoms of disease appeared in a procession of causes and effects, not one single doctor diagnosed them correctly.

The body language crying out for help is far more complicated than the study of physics. Einstein's principle of relativity, the cause and effect magic of science, is far easier to grasp than the language the body speaks when it tries to tell you what is wrong. Just as Einstein said that the universe is made up of very few principles, so are there very few principles you need to understand to get well and stay well. You are ill mostly because you have not found the source of who you are. The God of creation is waiting within, to guide the way and make your life complete; it is as simple as that.

The possibilities of stress being the cause of your symptoms need to be addressed. Symptoms with an emotional base can pathologically replicate real disease. I can personally testify that diabetes and all its attendant symptoms, including kidney and heart problems, can have a physical base as well as an emotional one. Diabetes can also be a compounding of a physical cause with a psychosomatic one. Stress can cause a heart attack, and then the stress of a heart attack itself can cause an overreaction that could cause death. One stress causes the problem, and the reaction to the symptom of stress can finish the job.

Then there are those psychosomatic disorders conveniently diagnosed as having a genetic or pathological base.

Treatments for the symptoms alone may temporarily relieve the patient of suffering, but in the end, the cause will manifest in other forms compounded by the side effects of the medication. And finally one can be so emotionally distressed and run down that the immune system is compromised, which then opens one to all manner of infections. The cost of so many medications may so impoverish people mentally, spiritually, as well as financially that they may have to choose between food and medication. Indeed many people live as empty shells waiting to die in some government or nursing home warehouse. What use is life without meaning, a live body with a dead spirit?

So if your sickness does not yield to conventional medicine, either one of two things is possible. The diagnosis and treatment is faulty, or your suffering problem is stress-based. It is also entirely possible that your illness is a combination of both the aforementioned factors. Which comes first, the chicken or the egg? Are you physically ill because of your emotions, with anger compounding the illness? Or do you have a physically-caused disease which you are compounding through frustration and emotional upset?

It's not unusual for people to have an accident on the job or in their automobile and to continue suffering from pain that no longer has any basis. The physical injury is healed, but the emotional wound, unforgiving with respect to the recall, causes the same reaction to the memory as if the accident were happening again and again; and so pain is the phantom of the original accident but emotionally sustained. If you should come to any harm, learn to deal with it with patience and equanimity. If you are resentful towards any injury, your body retains the memory and reproduces the symptoms upon being reminded and upset by observing similar circumstances.

Unforgiveness has an unusual way of coming back to mind for review. With that memory comes the image of the trauma and an opportunity to either renew your anger and unforgiveness toward it or let it go. Any traumatic event that manifests as disease or some behavior aberration can be kept alive, sustained without the memory coming to mind. You can bury the event, and then all that needs to happen for the behavior or the symptom to reappear is any kind of emotional upset. You see, resentment not only establishes trauma-based illnesses; it nurtures them. Resentment and anger cause you to remain run down and can keep lowering the resistance to diseases that flourish in an emotionally compromised immune system.

MISGUIDED FAITH

Remember the most dangerous emotional problem of all: placing your whole faith in medicine as a form of denial. People in denial are very strange creatures. Rather than admit their fault is spiritual, they will seek physical reasons to excuse it. If your faith is placed entirely in medicine, it becomes a religion, and then the hope of the cure is the real sickness. Don't get me wrong; you will need your doctor as your counselor and mechanic if need be. But quietly weigh the evidence and, for heaven's sake, use your own judgment. Get more than one opinion and discern for yourself with your God-given intuitive knowing.

With so many sick people and so much reliance on pharmaceutical marvels, doctors have so little time for each patient and even less to ferret out your dark secrets. And godless psychiatry will more often than not treat your emotional state with drugs. Any good psychiatrist will tell you that the hardest factor in treating patients is denial. Denial for most people is the drug of first choice. It is much easier for psychiatrists to help you live with your symptoms with their drugs than get you to face private demons.

People cling to their resentments, never realizing that hatred not only opens them up for the hell of life to penetrate them, it numbs the realization and the shame of a wasted life. In other words, emotion causes the problem and keeps you from seeing your wasted life.

There is a valid reason to probe your past for your emotional traumas. Your past sins and indiscretions have indeed caused your guilt, fears and anxieties. But the answers do not lie in the past; they have to do with dealing with emerging memories correctly in the present, or should I say The Eternal Ever Present. The now Presence is where one deals with the ghosts of past and future time.

Wisdom from the New Testament echoes like a haunting refrain, exhorting us to virtue through the centuries: one passage is especially valuable. "Resist not evil; overcome it with good." Unfortunately Bible translators did not always use the correct synonym. The synonym for resist is resent; now try reading the passage again, using resent instead of resist and see if this helps clarify the hidden meaning in the message. "Resent not evil;overcome it with good." You see, if you resent evil (in people), you are then separated from the good by which evil is overcome.

13

LIFE FORCE ORIGIN

Doctors, I must concede, have saved my life on two occasions. However, had they understood the subtle, and sometimes not-so-subtle, causes of disease, the monetary costs to me and my insurance company would have been significantly cheaper, and I would have experienced much less suffering.

Cause and effect relationships remain outside the area of focus for almost all doctors. They see disease—the visible sign of many causes and effects—as if it existed in isolation. And the medical community, with rare exceptions, attacks the symptom as though it were the cause. Doctors see themselves as heroic soldiers waging war on the body of effects. As a consequence, they will quickly point out, people do indeed live longer. The human body can be sustained through medical marvels, but those who do live longer only continue to worsen, and inevitably need another fix. And so disease, as well as the social problems caused by certain cures, becomes increasing complicated, and cries out for more marvels of medicine. Thus syphilis and gonorrhea cured are replaced by HIV, not so curable.

I am not a methodical, exhaustive researcher. Rather, my delight comes in seeking out those little nuggets of wonder researchers uncover. Science revels in empirical evidence; I take pleasure in what they fail to see. I look beneath their discovery to the cause. Einstein once said that the universe is made up of a very few principles; he wanted to know what God thought. My particular version of this principle lies in looking further and further back in time for the numen behind the phenomenon, seeking cause behind effects. I suppose if we were to go back far enough in time through all the causes and effects, we might discover the unprecedented impetus of all causes and effects. What better way to find the cause of all misery and suffering than by probing the failing of the human spirit—admittedly a dangerous practice.

THE FALLING

In exploring the origin of disease, I will endeavor to show that man has three distinct origins: one physical and environmental, the other two spiritual. Mankind has fallen victim to the mercy of nature, lured there by something sub-natural and unreal. Man has been created differently from all other creatures. He needs a master, a source of meaning and direction in his life. If he does not find and respond to the Creator source, then he is destined to continue responding not to the Creator but the creation, as an environmental source.

Both environments are grounds for being. In either case, mankind is compulsively shaped. Freedom does not exist in the sense in which it has always been conceived; there is a choice only between obedience to one realm or the other. The net result of not finding our spiritual origin, and hence our heavenly governance, is a conflict between what we are becoming, and what our potential for becoming is when found through our conscience. Our lives are lived within a war of the worlds, between dis-ease and harmony, good and evil.

I am choosing to explore the subject of cancer first for a good reason. It is one of those difficult and complicated illnesses that result from a long chain of causes and effects. By understanding each connecting link in a chain of causes and effects, we gain insights into most of human suffering.

For many years my intent has been to write a book about medicine, but only when I found the missing piece of a puzzle which has held me back, until now. I now know what that is. It has to do with character, or what some call "lifestyle." Admittedly, some diseases do not occur as the result of choices we consciously or unconsciously have made in our lives, and there is no fault associated with them. However, the great majority of diseases, mental, emotional, and physical, involve an unrecognized character flaw. This flaw has many branches, and they comprise most of our maladies. This hidden flaw is not psychological; it is an affliction of the soul.

Cancer as a disease has myriad manifestations. Some have nothing to do with a person's character or emotional circumstance. Too many sunburns at an early age, for example, may result in skin cancer, and require medical intervention. However, there are those forms of cancer that do indeed have a very deadly psychosomatic-emotional connection.

We must, in our examination of this disease, confront a phantom, a mysterious shadow that we cannot see, feel or ever touch. It can be seen only with the mind's eye. If we refuse

229

to be frightened by what is revealed, we will be able to watch the problem dissolve. With this in mind, let us explore the cause of one type of cancer and uncover all the symptoms we have ignored in our lives that have led to this disease, for most people live their lives like the driver who has disconnected that annoying engine warning light. Suddenly, things go wrong—too much at once for mechanics—or doctors.

THE BUSINESS FACE OF DISEASE

How different is the cancer found in the human body from the dysfunction we find in our society, in almost every facet, including, for example, business?

Something has gone wrong with your company. People are turning against you; your best employees are leaving. Your business is dying and you cannot figure it out. If you look very carefully you will discover that just one person is responsible. This individual has two faces: one for you, another for everyone else. More often than not, he or she is a skillful, apparently devoted friend who has worked his way into your confidence.

You will be hard pressed to fire or confront him, because he has wormed his way into your life and made himself essential to your business and personal life. You have become dependent in a very unhealthy way. This person is a cancer. At first you may not want to face what is going wrong. You may have even become comfortable. Certainly this person has not hesitated to make a home inside, displacing you to the extent that your whole world would fall apart were you to face this "friend," perhaps a member of your family.

Without consciously considering it, you sense the

230

problem, but your dependency makes you fearful of having the rug of security pulled from under you. Indeed it would be well and so much the better if you had the wisdom and fortitude for confrontation. There are no simple solutions to the problems of business, family or disease except by having a precise understanding of what the problem is and excising the offensive cause. With cancer and other forms of autoimmune problems, we have something akin to betrayal, something unholy sitting in the place of the holy.

Unless you first lay down the old life, you cannot pick up the new one. The good book says, "Who preserves his life shall lose it." This seems to say that if you cannot give up the old friend, you will not find the way that leads to eternal life. Eventually you will discover that if any of those seducers should die or openly betray you, you will surely feel that hollow at the core of your being.

Right here is a clue to one of those many causes and effects (symptoms-as-disease) underlying cancer. A gnawing feeling of insatiable hunger could be associated with a need for food, for which reason we become overweight and plagued by all the maladies associated with obesity. You compensate with food fulfillment, the nearest equivalent to soul food. Notice here the similarity to the comfort derived from a trusted friend. Notice also that your security is based upon the wrong kind of food, and right here you have the dietary cause for cancer.

Obviously food is not the real answer. Something much more vital than food is needed—the need for cruel or absent mother's love, perhaps? Even so, if you do excise certain people from your life or go on a diet, your need to gratify the ego self will take another form—you may start smoking. Your need for the comforter will attract you to similar types, cloaked in different disguises. And the resulting condition will always be worse than what came before; something inside is calling the shots.

If you are ready to continue this journey of self-discovery, freeze-frame the following statement. It will be paraphrased over and over again to emphasize a very important principle. In the late '60s, researchers revealed a connection between the loss of a loved one and the onset of cancer.

PSYCHIC VAMPIRES

A wonderful magic can be found in the way plants flower in the sun, the way one creature gives life to another. So it is in a different way with human life, with respect to our inner environment. Worldly experience should have told you by now that the way you exist has somehow gone wrong. Humans are indeed birthed like creatures of the animal kingdom. However, there is a difference to our ending. Instead of our lives simply ceasing to be, we alone can experience a new beginning—not merely sexually replacing our bodies, but becoming something far more beautiful.

Just as there are predators in the natural world, so there are predators lurking inside people. Relationships should be of a high ethical tone—spiritual—but more often than not they deteriorate, in both subtle and obvious ways, into a dog-eat-dog environment. People are predators as well as prey, with a kind of spiritual warfare going on. We must eventually transcend the malevolent influences of the world around us. We must find and bond with the true spiritual inner source of our identity, the first link in the causal chain. Without that mystical bonding, we are powerless before "the uninvited."

The natural world is inhabited by many kinds of parasites. Two-thirds of all living things are parasites, existing by preying upon others' lives. If this is true in the natural world, why should this not be true in the spiritual environment around us? We need to flush out the unseen parasitic forces lurking somewhere nearby us, hiding in the natural aspect of each and every one of us.

AN ALTERED ECOLOGY
CREATES A FISHY INSTABILITY

Changes in the environment create a variety of biological effects to which living things adapt. For example, fish caught in the polluted Santa Monica Bay were discovered to have large growths on their bodies, which were traced to a disturbance in the ecological balance of the water. Pollution had changed that balance. When the sustaining environment of a living thing is changed or removed, the identity of the life form is denied its security in more than one sense of the word. If a life form which falls victim to this change is unable to adapt quickly enough, a serious enervating reversal of its life-support system likely results. All living things must exist near their habitat, because their environment not only sustains their bodies, but also their identities. A subtle identity-sustaining essence emanates from the environment that is just as essential for the continuance of the creature's existence as food.

A certain kelp fish takes on the appearance of its environment. Not only does this environment serve as camouflage and food supply, it also provides for identity, the very core of the fish's existence. A person's relationship with others closely duplicates this principle, and is experienced as an emotional security. However, the problem with our emotional security is that there is nothing secure about it.

A closer look at our loss of security reveals an important point: any trauma or successful seduction tends to transfer your allegiance from your natural internal source of being to the violating one. Where you once were sovereign, you become slave. The violating source has become the ground of a new being within you. Unlike nature, which gives life in terms of food and identity, the seductive intelligence (the pseudonym for which is temptation) reverses the process of nature. It draws you away from your true identity and feeds off your need, your weakness. The tiny psychic earthling displacing your soul cries out for mothering, for a sense of completeness and fulfillment.

The kind of person who violates and sucks energy from your life usually has little or no life force of his or her own. For the sake of identity and a sense of wholeness, you find yourself giving up more and more of your real life, mistaking that giving to be love and devotion. This lifestyle leads to illness and your early demise. You are literally empowering your environment to kill you. Until you understand all this, you will go on giving your life in exchange for the ego illusion of worth. Plain and simple, your phony friend is a spiritual vampire.

Whether excited by the eerie presence of what seems to be fulfilling love or outraged by overt cruelty and manipulating skills, you exude an unhealthy vitality upon which the parasite psychically feeds. Such vampires always walk away strengthened by the encounter, while you feel drained. Stop and think for a moment. How many different illnesses can you name that are the result of the lack of motivation and

234

energy? So wake up, use your God-given common sense and perceptive powers, and you will see all those who drain you. You cannot live with these people; nor can you live without them. You need to find a much higher source of love and life-giving fulfillment which gives you His life form in exchange for your devotion. This life you seek is not of this world; it awaits within. If you are willing to find God in your heart, then be still and you will know Him.

LIFE SUCKS

All morbid thought originates from the same source. The nature that has made a home in you has bond-slaved you to the environment of the "friendly" alien. Having recreated the brainchild of itself inside you, it is now slowly but surely transforming you into its likeness. Your consciousness, instead of being objectively in control, is struggling, caught up in a whirlpool of negativity. In much the way that iron filings reveal the outline of a magnetic field, so does the implanted identity draw negative destructive thoughts around itself. It makes you crave the vampire's love, which requires you to remove the proverbial garland of garlic and protective crucifix from around your neck. In exchange for this gesture of acceptance, you receive the kiss of death, paid with your lifeblood. Consider now whether or not you have an unhealthy fascination for death with a Dracula in your life. In Bram Stoker's story of the undead, Dracula offers an infernal life as though it were the eternal one. The victim exchanges her real substance and life force for the strange vainglorious identity of the undead.

Pardon the analogy, but something similar is going on in

almost everyone's life. That's why life sucks. Another identity is appropriating your immune system for itself. This is the reason I believe that in order to fight cancer, medical science currently relies on an approach that must first kill the immune system. More likely than not, this is the underlying principle behind most autoimmune diseases. Long before the malignancy appears, it will have already compromised your immune system and produced symptoms that you ignored or treated too lightly, often with over-the-counter medicine. All over-reactions cause enervation that emotionally compromises the immune system and invites in virus-based illnesses and disease.

The conflict of not being true to ourselves is the root of most drug and alcohol problems. Psychologically, it is a war between what we are becoming, and what our conscience is trying to tell us to be. Here once more is the familiar pattern. We met the enemy—it is us.

14

RECLAIMING YOUR
IMMUNE SYSTEM

If you were to fight a war, you would be sure to have enough tanks, guns, ammunition, airplanes and battleships to ensure a victory over your enemy. Being a peaceful person and not the aggressor, you would use all the implements of warfare only as a defense. This strategy also works for your immune system; it needs to be mobilized, always healthy and fine tuned, ready to fight disease and viruses.

Then again, wars are fought on different levels, not just with guns and soldiers against guns and soldiers. The enemy tries to penetrate your defenses with his intelligence and undermine your war effort with sabotage, to weaken morale. He will send spies to steal your secret weapons, and most dangerous of all, his tactic is to place one of his "moles" in your highest level of command.

Fighting virus and bacteriological warfare requires you to have all your ducks in a row. What I mean is that you must be spiritually, psychologically, emotionally and physically fine-tuned. It is all very well to eat sensibly, take your vitamins and all that good stuff, but if you are emotionally upset all the time, your immune system is undermined and compromised by the enemy. If the secret cause that allows for disease is not detected and remedied, the positive value of your food and that healthier lifestyle is diminished.

FRIENDLY ENEMIES

I have a saying, "live longer, become wronger," which means that if you are overreacting and losing control over your life, you have allowed an enemy into your camp, thus undermining your war effort, so to speak. Your emotional reactions to stress allow the enemy to penetrate your defenses on a spiritual, psychological and emotional level. And if you were fighting a real war with a visible enemy, you would, as a good commander-in-chief, pay much attention to internal security.

But do we look inwardly? And even if we do look inside and understand what our problem is, we may overreact and become overly focused, distracted and dangerously absorbed there. However, if we have the proper insight and resolve, we will inherit the natural power to fight a unified war on all fronts and win. The first enemy you must deal with is your own private demon.

The enemy has gotten inside, and like the Trojan horse, will open the gates of the city to your enemy. I know it is difficult to look at the enemy within and see what a fool you have been, especially if it's in the guise of "love and friendship."

The chances are that the very fact that you are sick in the first place could mean that your enemy has already penetrated your defenses on a spiritual, psychological, and/or emotional

238

level and has compromised your immune system. Yes, of course you need doctors to help treat the symptom, but you must not put all your faith in medicine: do not make doctors your God. Putting all your faith in doctors will unbalance your faith in God and reset the stage for your next suffering. By allowing the doctor to release you from your responsibility for your own suffering, you set him up to fail. In this way you unconsciously cause the cure to become the sickness. In a sense, you have made an enemy out of what might have been a friend. By misusing the doctor's services, you begin to rely on the medicine rather than on strengthening your own immune defenses.

Even the most well-meaning physician with his most excellent science can become your betrayer, not always because he intends to hurt you, but because the doctor himself is subject to the same system to which you are subject, which means that neither one of you understands the real problem. Your physician's own training has betrayed him, something he may one day have to face. Many wise doctors realize later in life that medicine is only half of the answer. You see, the entire human race is in the same boat.

MEDICINE'S MISSING LINK

Most doctors are compassionate, decent people who want to alleviate the suffering they see all around them in any way they can. The problem is that they are taught to see the symptom as the cause. There are many reasons why people elect to become doctors. It could be for example, a traumatic experience in a person's life: seeing a loved one die in agony from cancer, and resolving there and then, that since God does

239

not answer prayers, he will better God and fight the scourge of disease himself. Some wannabe physicians work only for the sake of power, money and ambition. Physicians such as these are not teachable; they rarely become wise. Some of these doctors are threatened by real cures.

Then there is a certain type of woman who chooses nursing as a profession because of a submissive relationship with her sick mother. Her angry and sick mother always made her feel guilty and responsible for her unhappiness and illness, so the daughter became devoted to serving her mother out of guilt until the old girl died. Feeling that void which comes from being compelled to serve out of guilt, and having become addicted to the role of slave, she turned to the nursing profession. Without understanding what had happened to her, she tended to become the enabler with all her patients.

I don't mean to impugn the character of all health professionals because their remedies can be extremely valuable, but without the modifying factor of enlightened reason, they simply become part of the patient's problem. There are many well-meaning physicians and health practitioners who are beginning to see the failing one-sided approach to medicine. Antibiotics are failing and germ and virus strains are becoming dominant once again. We could very well be facing a pandemic of frightening proportions. The symptom-as-the--cause approach to medicine is dangerously flawed. If you are ever to recover from what is, or could become, a terminal illness, you must see the truth about this lie. Faith in the efficacy of medicine as the cure is equivalent to Adam's doubt that separated him from the Paradise state. Doubting the truth transfers one's loyalty to the lie. Faith in the deceiver transfers from the immortal to a mortal with a slavish trust in the misuse of every kind of help.

240

THE SENSUAL WAR WITH THE SENSIBLE

Know that when you believe the lie, you are compelled to doubt the common sense of truth you were born with. Doubting what is true in your heart delivers you to the enemy, which then becomes the subtle root of all manner of suffering. To doubt what you know is right in your heart is to believe into, and become addicted to, the consolation of the lie. From the lie believed, a spirit enters, and from that springs anxiety, guilt, tension, and depression, which in turn begin to make "you" look outwardly to compensate for what you've lost inwardly. You seek the lost love, security, happiness, salvation and eventually health in all the wrong places, making the same mistake of placing your trust in well-meaning as well as dishonest people, over and over again. Unfortunately, the stubbornness of your ego, unable to face the truth of its failing, continues to seek comfort from the friendly enemies and to turn friends into enemies, setting them up to fail you.

Remember, the lie you have accepted implants an identity that slowly takes shape in you, which then becomes the spy in your midst as in real warfare. It seems like one of yours when it's really one of them. And from its home in you it signals its need for support. Unconsciously you will be drawn to the kind of person in your past that got past your defense through some distant trauma of failing. Nearly all your friends and helpers will nurture the enemy within who will weaken your defenses and eventually betray you to disease and suffering.

The friend you marry becomes the fiend you divorce. What you call love and attraction becomes rage and frustration, eventually soothed by the company that alcohol and drugs keep. The external conflict intensifies the psychological and physical distress call, and their cry for relief invites the world in. Does not your Bible tell you that the love of the world is at enmity with God? In your fallen state, the truth is evermore threatening, while the lie is increasingly and sensuously reassuring the ego.

Herbal remedy food fads and diets, in fact, all the things that might do you some good have a diminishing value with respect to your unresolved internal problem. For example, if you have a parasite such as an amoeba or tapeworm in your intestine, all the remedies in the world will not help much until you excise the cause. Then remedies can help you recover. However, most of the time we are not dealing with actual physical causes that do have physical remedies. Fully 80 percent of most illnesses, mental, emotional and physical, are what is called psychosomatic. Psychosomatic illness is thought to be the effect that the mind has on the body. Here again experts have missed the point.

STRUGGLE FEEDS THE ILLNESS

That the mind disturbs bodily functions is only partly true. I pointed out earlier in this work that the soul should be sovereign over the mind, emotions and body; unfortunately it is not. The reason is that the spirit has lost its connection to God. The evidence of this division is that the body reacts compulsively to the will lurking behind all forms of stress, and the reaction always expresses itself in emotion. Emotion in turn translates into negative thoughts and pulls the consciousness into a whirlpool of thinking helplessly. Here we witness two struggles. The first struggle is with the external adversary. We overreact and lose. Overreacting opens the gates of our mind and allows the enemy in to torment and confuse our soul

242

from its base in our thinking. If we struggle with our thoughts and feelings, we notice that we use up our resources fighting, eventually giving in, thereby making our internal problem worse as the extension of our external problems.

THE POWERLESS ADVERSARY

What I'm saying here is that if you do not have enough power to fight the enemy, you do not have sufficient tanks and guns and airplanes, and so the enemy defeats you and takes the spoils of victory, your life force. So you become feebler and it becomes stronger. Somehow you must find the strategic spiritual ally which you presently do not know anything about. I say this because we are not fighting what appears to be the enemy. We are struggling with something far more subtle. The force we are fighting has no real power of its own. It literally seduces you, tricks you out of your power, and uses it against you. It intimidates you to resist its superior will with your puny one; it needs you to be upset and struggle with it because it knows you will lose to it. You will exhaust yourself struggling, making yourself sicker, intensifying your thirst for food, wine, women and song. Eventually you will give in to its greater calling. This losing struggle also holds true on a cellular level. Fear not; I will show you where your own source of power waits inside you, and when you learn how to resist without overreacting, you will rob the enemy of his power. Perhaps you understand better now that the spirit of evil has seduced the entire world, exchanging the paradigm of heaven for that of hell. This transfer of authority is accomplished when you are tricked into doubting the truth in your heart and trusting in the lie.

243

With certain forms of cancer, the invader appropriates the immune system. You may not know that the invader is there because it thinks it is you and you think it is it. The inner sanctum has been compromised at the highest level of spirit; it is in command of your natural forces. Your own body cells are dispirited. Some cells begin to respond to the invader and your body responds in a way that traumatizes the resisting cells, bidding them to give up and conform just as you have done in your life in relating to other people. The conforming cell becomes a change agent enemy of the healthy cells that finally also change sides through having tried to resist without the power to do so. As the result of the struggle and enervation of life force, the whole body feeds itself to the sickness and you die. You die two deaths, one of the body, preceded by that of the spirit.

Think of this process in a new light; think of the struggle as a form of denial. You need the challenge, the struggle to puff up your pride, and you need it as a distraction from the guilt of being proud. You are struggling without the ennobling power of faith that would quiet your perverse need for distraction. The adversary provides cruelty and injustice as a tease offering for your ego, causing it to puff up like a cobra with judgment. You think you're dealing with a person; instead, it is a spirit using a corrupted human form to penetrate you in the same way that it has been corrupted by other "changed" agents. Your disenfranchised spirit, your ego, is no match for such temptation. But in your pride you rise to every challenge and continue to fall and fail in a vicious, self-destructive cycle.

There are those who would rather reign in hell than serve in heaven.

Resentment is your Achilles heel; resentment is anger, the handmaiden of judgment. While the bully is addicted to power, you have also become addicted by judging and using judgment of his evil as food for your continuing judgment. Without grace, your naive spirit will always succumb to the seasoned victim who has turned bully. Resentment and hostility toward others can turn inward toward you. If you don't turn your anger inward, you will become a change agent and take it out on your family and people weaker than yourself, thereby impregnating them with the spore of the alien spirit which you carry. You may not get ulcers, but you give them, if you see what I mean. Really wicked people rarely get really sick. Why is this, you ask? It is because they had no guilt for stealing from others what was taken from them. Because he is ruthless enough through degrading others for their life force, just one such outrageous individual can stay healthy on a diet of frightened victims.

THE VAMPIRE BULLY

When one gives out life force to another individual, two failings are involved. One failing is that of the victim who gives up life and power. The other failing is that of the tormentor who comes down from his sovereignty to soak up that power and becomes addicted, ever more ruthless for the sake of that power. Victims, having sacrificed their power, often turn around and take it out on others in a military chain of command; the victim is drained of power and in exchange becomes impregnated with the alien spirit. Powerless, but weak before the strong, they become strong before the weak. The coward becomes the bully and feeds his alien identity with the life force of those he seeks to torment. In every people-pleasing coward lurks the seed of a vampire bully.

The life force of an entire nation can be siphoned all the way up to the top, to the chief despot, while the identity of his evil nature travels down the chain of command of authority to all the citizens, infecting a multitude of people exponentially. Eventually an entire nation can become death-centered through its leader, as it was with Hitler's Germany and Stalin's Russia. All change agents are addicted to brutality and cruelty, with higher and higher degrees of violence according to rank in order to extract the life force, which they must inevitably yield up to their immediate superiors. So it comes to pass with the nation as with the body on the cellular level. Democracies have surrendered their sovereignty to usurping tyrants, as do cells to the usurping cancer personality that has ascended unholy to the place of the holy, like a political monster with an insatiable appetite for power. If Adolf Hitler had not been able to feed his perverse appetite for power from his soldiers' ravaging of conquered nations, his bloodlust would have fallen upon his own people until there was no one left to drink. Make no mistake; the purpose of cruelty and violence is spiritual vampirism.

15

The Secret Cause
of Cancer

IDS: IDENTITY DISPLACEMENT SYNDROME

Solving the riddle of cancer is like assembling the pieces of a jigsaw puzzle. If one has all the pieces or at least most of them, it's only a matter of collation and then observing for any missing parts. I believe my calling allows me to take any of the acceptable discoveries of science and come to some different conclusions based on the evidence. The conclusion here is that a certain type of cancer can result from a form of possession, incurable without recognizing and confronting the real invisible enemy within.

Some people, including many eminent scientists and researchers, will never confront an alternate reality, preferring instead the security of their own failing one. Denial is a pervasive, all-too-human propensity that lies at the heart of all human suffering and tragedy.

Why do some cancers go mysteriously into remission,

while others do not? Perhaps the difference is an individual spiritual one, beyond the grasp of any contemporary religion and science. The cause of many illnesses lies in the soul, beyond the scope of godless psychiatry. Some diseases are simply environmental, while others have a spiritual component that lie at their root. Everything wrong needs to be made right at its root. Cancer is one of those diseases that can have both physical and spiritual aspects.

The problem with most sciences, especially in physics, medicine and cellular biology, is that researchers tend to come to only one conclusion, which is that they see everything as having a physical cause and effect origin. I certainly have no argument with physical causes becoming effects and continuing as links in a causal chain; that is just plain common-sense science.

However, we ought not to always approach problems from the strictly scientific viewpoint. There are at least two exceptions to this rule. The first is that the universe needs to be the effect of a non-material uncaused cause, an unmoved mover, a metaphysical or spiritual cause of all physical cause and effect phenomena. And the second related mystery is that man appears to have originated differently from all other creatures, and that he too had a timeless metaphysical spiritual origin from which (by choice) he fell away. It is from this assumption that I will make my case for the cause and cure of cancer. Kindly bear with me as I lay down a philosophical foundation, a bridge between two worlds.

THE ORIGIN OF BIOLOGICAL CHAOS

Man obviously possesses a conscious-spiritual choice, in contrast to the instinctual reflexes of animals. That conscience

248

is what distinguishes man from beast. Through conscience, mankind is gifted with a mysterious choice factor. Choice sets before us two very extreme outcomes. There is a subtle reason why we are provided this conscious destiny of choice. When our Creator desired to create true love, He did so in the only way possible—with the freedom to choose Him, for such love could never be compelled. Freedom from reality can only come from also creating another opposing illusory reality, which world could be entered by choice.

Most young people seem to be cursed with the belief that they are gods and hence immortal. Perhaps it is true that we are all afflicted with the inherent legacy of Adam. Remember how the first man was deceived into eating the fruit of rebellion, seduced into believing he was equal with God and would never die. Perhaps the wild and irresponsible behavior of many young people may be caused by that (inherent) ego sense of godly immortality. If this were so, then their every choice would lead away from good to ever more desperate ego choices, until it came time for that proverbial wake-up call. Does the morass of suffering always awaken people from their nightmare dream existence? The answer is, rarely. There is a saying that God's love gives freedom, but from the devil's love, there is no escape. Compulsion and addiction are a faithless clinging to the security of an inherited alternate reality—that stubborn, egotistic, earth-bound devotion to the dark side of the force.

CHOOSING CHOICE: ORIGINAL SIN?

The idea of choice being a divine right is still very appealing to the egos of those who need justification for their misbegotten existence. Pro-choice advocates are easily deluded into thinking that the factor of choice is itself a virtue, when it is a means to a very bad end.

You might well ask, if choices are inherent and compulsive, where's the choice? The answer to that is that you still have not used up your choice between good and evil. For contemporary man, it is whether or not to be saved from the inherent ego hell of compulsive choosing. Some people solve this problem by fearing to make decisions and letting others make decisions for them.

The freedom to choose is a dimensional exercise of will that allows us to determine our destiny. The freedom to choose has to do with relationship, with respect to who or what we serve; it is not the freedom we want it to be. Choice is a matter of allegiance; through stubbornness you remain in denial, as a fool, unknowingly a change agent for evil. Anytime you are ready to awaken, you can exercise your choice and surrender your pride in humility to God. You see, it's not really a choice; it is more a salvation from all the slavish "choices" that you have inherited.

It is good to be mindful of your mortality as a precaution against becoming so high that your ego might dare to think there are no consequences. The prerogative of any god is choice; it is a god whose choices can never be wrong, support for which is always precisely where every seducer makes his or her approach. Every pressure or enticement to enable you to make that (selfish) choice is a little slice of death.

Before us lies, in those two paths, two kinds of freedom: continued freedom from right to do wrong, and freedom (salvation) from wrong to do what the inner wordless guiding light shall reveal. License is the seducer's kind of freedom, which through a little experience exposes itself for what it really is: slavery, self-destruction and eventually chaos that extends down even to the cellular level.

The spirit of the world licenses you to live out what appears to be a self-serving existence with every right to choose becoming the "right" in itself, an entitlement, a glorious unalienable liberty. Eventually, you may learn that you are "growing" in the way you are going, slowly transformed into a deformed likeness you have unconsciously loved and embraced. As the good book says, "what is seen is made by what does not appear." So take a good hard look in the mirror.

You did not consciously choose the misfortune of ill health, calamity and premature death; you merely continued in the legacy of giving way, selfishly, to all the wrong impulses. Your problem is one of ego, which falsely believes it is doing its own thing and prides itself in its rebellion against the salvation of common sense; until this state of mind is remedied, you will continue to be drawn into all the wrong influences.

Pro-choicers having succumbed to temptation and, angry over the outcome of their promiscuous pleasure-taking, open themselves up to the second level of descent, again the lie that choice is some kind of divine right. Wrong choices continue to lead to the desperation of choices and blame. Anger toward the innocent unborn for "ruining their lives" renders souls suggestible to that lying way out, which is that "choice" means "the right to choose," and the belief that this right in itself is what Right is. This may well be true between chocolate ice cream and vanilla, but not for whether a baby lives or dies. You may have perhaps noticed how outraged these people become when confronted with the issue. It is as though you questioned God. Such people always stand reason on its head.

We all have a choice to steal, murder, rape, pillage and plunder, but is it right to do such things? What if we all believed the way pro-choicers do? There would be chaos, as indeed exists in many countries.

There are no choices and no chaos in the animal realm; they are chained as prescribed by instinct. No creature can be anything more than what it was created to be. For all living things, there is only a physical life and a physical death, but for humans there is an eternal or an infernal one with a hellish glimpse of a reality to come.

The path you have been unwittingly following invites chaos. Should you survive the ravages of a misguided existence and live long enough, you will most likely die from the cell chaos known as cancer. Lifestyle choices submerge your body into union with various environmental carcinogenic chemicals, especially with regard to food.

Earlier, I laid the foundations for the spiritual root cause of cancer. The cancer personality is drawn to everything that is wrong—wrong friends, wrong food, wrong remedies—and so adapts to an unnatural and poisonous environment. You may see this phenomenon in others but not yourself, because of a denial factor. If you are falsely secure in your choices, you will never see anything wrong with your lifestyle. And when things go awry, as they inevitably will, you tend to blame (another bad choice) and begin responding to the very poisonous circumstances you projected. You bump into a chair and you cry, "oh, that stupid chair," when it's you who is stupid, but you cannot see it because your focus is on blaming the chair.

And so most of us go through life becoming angrier and angrier at everything that goes more and more wrong, justifying failing through anger that also poisons. Anger, like excessive pleasure, emotionally bonds you environmentally to the aggravatingly seductive hate object. Physical addictions are a good example.

You are trying to quit smoking and you find that the more you try, the more you fail. In a sheer exercise of will, you keep on trying, but you keep on failing. The very effort of your will gives strength to the habit you are fighting. Your body has just so many defenses and cannot indefinitely survive the environment of poisons into which you are drawn, mind and body, and then something has to change.

At some point you will be unable to throw off the now invasive carcinogenic poison of nicotine because it has become psychologically and environmentally compatible with "your" (it's not you) need to numb reality and assuage the conflict of your failing life. You might not be so affected by secondhand smoke were you not so aggravated and sensitized by the obnoxious and inconsiderate behavior of smokers at home or at work.

THE ONCOLOGY OF THE UNHOLY SPIRIT

There is a spiritual, psychological reason why the survival rate of two people in the same poisonous environment differs. The angry person absorbs noxious poisons, while more balanced individuals develop their natural resistance. Anger and resentment separate you from your indwelling good and open the door to the "uninvited" nature whose comfort lies in poison. The drug addict is absorbed into an environment of poison as well as with noxious people providing for their "security." In this light it would be wise to take another look at all those forbidden foods you can't resist and know are bad for you. There must be a very long list of carcinogenic junk

253

foods you compulsively shove down your gullet to assuage anxiety whenever you are frustrated and upset. Cancer of the colon and stomach, anyone?

Food can serve to energize the good nature in us or the other, egomaniacal nature. Our relationship with food becomes carcinogenic when it is used as a drug. This is to say that we tend to "get into" food as a form of comfort and security the way a drug addict does. In this fashion, food fails to truly nourish your body and serve the good in your soul. The seductive chemistry of forbidden food fuses your ego to your body on a cellular, environmental level, changing your soul's pattern of growth from the true master builder's direction. Habit and different forms of self-abuse affect the location of symptoms.

In certain regions of Africa, a steady diet of vegetables and grains ensure that the inhabitants enjoy one-tenth the rate of the colon cancer of the West. In other locations of Africa, liver cancer is 18 times higher than in Great Britain. In Japan, the stomach cancer rate is 11 times that of the United States. And in the United States, the colon cancer rate is 20 times that of those living in certain parts of Africa. So what is your poison?

You may realize that you are on a terrible diet, but find yourself unable to recognize what a good diet is. Which of 5000 different diet schemes can you trust and follow? And even if you found the perfect diet, would you be able to follow it and stomach what is good for you? You see the problem, don't you? Like any addict, the alien self is addicted to the forbidden fruits, the various toxic environmental securities, in the form of mind-numbing carcinogens, essential to the construction of its rebellious existence.

All growth requires stimulation signals, whether internally positive or tragically traumatic. Cellular growth is the end product of a long complex process of "decisions" both psychological and physical. There is only so much the body can do to throw off wrong reactions and defend itself from deliberate exposure to toxic human and chemical elements, and sooner or later it will adapt to the stress source for survival, and then the first renegade immortal cell appears.

Cancer cells develop as the result of a series of multiple steps that could be described as Darwinian mutation, a repeated round of traumatic mutations followed by selection (of the renegade cell). The mutant cell would bear the genetic blueprint of the overshadowing (deformed) master builder spirit to which it has conformed.

Mankind is indeed made in the image of God, mortal by way of the first man's falling away and seeking that elusive status such as God might have; otherwise, he (Adam) might have been truly body and soul perfect and immortal. Alas, the spirit of seduction that we inherit is mortal, and belatedly eternal. Bearing witness to the governing overriding spirit, the mutant cell bears witness in the flesh to the disheveled alien image of paradise lost.

Wherever tumors emerge, they take on the appearance of alien life forms—the unseen and the uninvited that entered through the portal of the rebellious spirit, and which through stealth begin their program of destruction from within. Evil cannot create an original human to service its purpose on earth as it is in Hades; the best it can do is seduce and take over God's creature and express its immortal will through that stolen form.

255

Mutant cells are "immortal," while normal cells are not. Normal cells, when placed in a petri dish of nutrient, will double a limited number of times and then slowly die. But mutant cells will double without limit and without design and never die, representing, I believe, the infernal immortality of the ominous presence it represents.

Tumors themselves are not the foreign invaders; they are formed from the same material used by the body to construct its own tissues. The jumbled mass of biological disorder cannot be cured by medicine alone. The cure requires getting all your ducks in a row. The first duck is right attitude, which is to say right standing with God, a submission to his will to cast out the impostor.

The external factors affecting your health—lifestyle, diet, and environment—while they play an enormous role in determining the onset of disease and its location, by themselves can at best only delay an early demise; however there is an exception. While environment is an essential cancer causative factor, cancer does not necessitate spiritual character factor. For the more balanced and innocent person, a change of circumstance, diet and some medical intervention may effect a cure.

You see, don't you, how stubbornness and unrepentant attitude can lock a person into the various poisonous lifestyles? We are all sooner or later immersed in the lifestyles of others. Personally, I was forced to work in a sweatshop as a lad of 14 years of age, in an environment of filthy language and foul air polluted by cigarette smoke. A person of my awareness conspires to escape such an environment, but even if I were unable, that environment would not have permanently affected me as much as those kind of people who spawned it.

The various plagues that have ravaged the human race

from time to time do not kill everyone. Appearance, age or personality never reveal the noble ones deserving of survival. It is also a mystery as to why some people can receive this kind of message with joy and others with anger and disbelief.

The predisposition to cancer that runs in families may have very little to do with genetics per se. More likely it is the environmental transfer of identity through a seductively cruel and unhealthy emotional climate. A young girl might take on the identity of her overbearing mother, for instance. And to the degree that the transference is completed, to that degree will she have exactly the same symptoms—cancer or other identity-based illnesses. And even if the transfer of identity is imperfect, you may have experienced the vague feeling that you are going to die at a certain age, and from the same malady your parent died of.

Earlier I suggested that the reason why medicine needs to destroy the immune system in order to cure cancer is because the patient's compromised immune system has been corrupted to serve the alien identity lurking in the unconscious. Wrong choices and many denials introduce repeated rounds to mutation, ending in the cellular oncology of the unholy spirit.

Discovering that one has a terminal illness such as cancer ought to be grounds for a wake-up call and a reality check. The difference between those whose cancer goes into remission permanently and those who go from bad to worse, regardless of apparent heroics, is usually a covert unwillingness to face the truth of their secret failing life. Many people would rather be dead than admit they are wrong. Denial is the last and worst decision that such people will ever make. Any attempt to hold up the truth to people in denial is like holding up a cross to a vampire.

If you ask me what the mystery is concerning those who turn to the light and those who continue towards darkness and death, I would tell you that I do not know the answer. Choice does exactly what it is meant to do. Choice gives Adam's progeny their choice, the way out, the opportunity to be saved by the grace of the God who made us, or continue eating the forbidden fruits, choosing to sustain the inherent delusion, sustaining that ego status such as a God might have.

The ego sees itself as the center of everything, a God always and never wrong no matter what it does. Fallen from God's love and having no life force of its own, it seeks power, glory and the enslaving worship of others. Beware of those self-centered, self-serving souls as they lie on their deathbed. Only those who are very close to such a person can know what they are really like and how they have a subtle and saccharin way of aggravating servitude, sucking the life force from those around them.

Those timid souls who sacrifice themselves seeking that brownie button of approval are in grave danger. So are those who live under circumstances where they are compelled to submit to syrupy sweet tyranny. Children may die from a different form of cancer: leukemia, doting parents not as sweet as they appear. Cancer personalities have no life force of their own; they acquire life force by seducing those around them from God's light, to see them as that light, and in doing so cause them to give up their vital forces.

A demanding mother, who succeeds in eliciting a life-long compulsive servitude from her daughter, can transfer her malignant personality to her offspring before she dies, leaving behind her hell's replacement.

258

CELLULAR MULTIPLICATION:
WINNING THROUGH INTIMIDATION

Have you ever experienced tyranny, living with a despotic, overbearing, manipulating spouse, lover, father, or brother perhaps? If you have, you may have experienced the frustration of giving in for peace and never ever finding it; instead you find yourself feeding your life to the tyrant empowering him or her to torment you even more. Perhaps you did not succumb to appeasing the tyrant, but you observed the dominating personality rewarding others for their servility.

What happens between people is precisely duplicated in our body when the intimidating renegade mutant cell first appears amidst your member cells. The intimidating, dominant mutant causes the surrounding cells to overreact and hence give up their life force to it. There is a two-way transfer occurring here. The intimidating personality, while causing a reaction in its hapless victim cells, implants its foreign agenda, while at the very same moment sucking up power from the victim. The victim's loyalty is converted and becomes the extension of the mutant personality, changing it to a mutant cell. The tyrant cancer on society is merely the macrocosm of which the body politic is a reflection.

ABOUT THE AUTHOR

Roy Masters—who in his 80s continues to broadcast the longest-running counseling show in talk radio history—started his journey toward understanding human nature in the most unlikely of places.

Growing up in pre-WWII England, one day as a teen he walked through a vaudeville show in the south coast town of Brighton, when a stage hypnotist caught his eye. He watched, fascinated, as the performer easily put his volunteer subjects under a hypnotic spell and induced each of them to do strange and outlandish things, like dancing around the stage with a broom, and forgetting their own names.

How, the young Roy wondered, could a smiling, personable stranger cause well-dressed, educated, competent adults to forget their names? Puzzled by the mysterious power the hypnotist had exercised over his subjects, Roy distinctly remembers pondering the question: "<u>Why can't hypnotism</u> <u>be used to make people act sensibly, rather than foolishly?</u>" <u>Inspired by the idea of harnessing this baffling force for</u>

good, he later pursued the art of hypnotism and established a successful hypnotherapy practice.

It was during those years of practicing hypnosis therapeutically, however, that Masters made his central and pivotal discovery about the nature of human beings' emotional problems, addictions and complexes.

As clinical psychologist Ron Carlson, Ph.D., would later describe this breakthrough: "Roy Masters' books reveal with penetrating insight that, unbeknownst to most of us, we are tethered to our thoughts in a destructive, hypnotic way which forms the basis of our emotional and mental problems."

In other words, Masters had discovered that people didn't really need hypnosis, because their core problem was that they were *already hypnotized*—not by a clever stage performer, but by the stresses, pressures and seductions of daily life. After all, it stood to reason that whatever little-understood forces were at play on a hypnotist's stage must also exist in real life as well. Virtually everyone, it turns out, is far too easily influenced by the intimidation, impatience and cruelty of other people, which in turn reprograms them in negative and destructive ways.

Over years of counseling as well as personal experience, Roy realized that the root of the power of negative suggestion lay in our wrong emotional response, and so he began to search for a way to help people overcome the hypnotic power of stress. After years of searching, he discovered a remarkably effective meditation method, and has been teaching it—with spectacular results—ever since.

This "meditation exercise"—a simple observation technique called *Be Still & Know,* from the Psalm verse, "Be still and know that I am God"—is at the core not only of Masters' unmatched track record in helping people overcome even the most serious mental-emotional problems, but now comprises the centerpiece of a successful program within the U.S. military ("Patriot Outreach") that is helping thousands of U.S. military personnel and their families to overcome the ravages of post-traumatic stress disorder (PTSD).

Roy counsels people primarily through his internationally syndicated daily radio program *Advice Line,* where callers discuss their most intimate problems and find genuine help and healing. For over 50 years, Roy has served as a daily voice of sanity and conscience to his listeners, with the uncanny ability to zero in quickly on core problems and help people take charge of their own lives.

As the institutional home for his counseling work, Masters' formed the Foundation of Human Understanding, a nonprofit 501(c)(3) organization, in 1961. Through his daily radio broadcasts, lectures, seminars, his 18 books, countless audio and video programs—and now, over the Internet—he has helped millions worldwide, including many celebrities like the late John Wayne, extricate themselves from vexing personal problems, substance abuse and emotional traumas. He has also established a successful prison outreach and an innovative private K-12 school.

Beyond all this, and at a time in life when most people would have long since retired, an energetic Roy Masters is delving deeply into yet another long-time interest—physics and cosmology. He has authored "Finding God in Physics" as well as a more technical treatise, "Gravity Driven Universe" and has lectured on "Electricity from Gravity" at the American Physical Society in Denver.

Roy Masters and his wife, Ann, have been married since 1952. They have five grown children and 18 grandchildren and great-grandchildren.

. .I must say; on the basis of 20 years experience, that the application of this technique has made a significant contribution to the treatment of the great majority of those people who have learned it. Particularly gratifying has been the experience with those individuals, actually quite numerous, who do not seem to benefit from classical analytically oriented psychotherapy; but who through the process of meditation do begin to develop insight into their difficulties and thereby a new sense of control over their lives.

In closing, I would like to add a personal note of thanks to Roy Masters for his generosity and encouragement in the application of his techniques to medical practice.

Dr. George M. Hayter, Psychiatrist
Chairman, Department of Psychiatry
St. Joseph's Hospital, Orange, California

Beyond Socrates, beyond Freud, Roy Masters brings you face to face with the reality of your own being. Will you dare to see the truth?

Engaging, revolutionary, and humorous, this book, like no other, can lead you to see your own deepest secrets. What was baffling will become dear. What created pain will provide joy. Roy Masters is a living spiritual giant whose words reawaken you to the truth contained in the depths of your own being.

Teresa Bahder, M.A.
Clinical Psychologist
Princeton, New Jersey

It is not unusual for great achievers to go unrecognized by the age in which they live. Such will be the case with the work of Roy Masters and the organization that houses the fruit of his life, The Foundation of Human Understanding.

Today precious few see the miracle of the availability of clear, unambiguous answers to life's major questions; answers hidden from human access for a millennia or more. I have found no other who speaks, as Roy Masters does, to the growing pain trapped in the breast of every soul, crying in hundreds of languages, forms and expressions: "Who am I and why was I born? Is there really a God and order to this chaos? What about the horror that has become my life? Why am I so confused, afraid?"

Emanuel McLittle, MA.
Counseling Psychologist

Roy Masters' books reveal with penetrating insight that, unbeknownst to most of us, we are tethered to our thoughts in a destructive, hypnotic way which forms the basis of our emotional and mental problems. Just as unknown to us are the spiritual and psychological ramifications of that entranced relationship with our thinking. Roy shows us that nothing less than extricating ourselves from our unconscious state of mind and suggestive state of soul can save us from the tragic consequences unfolding in our lives. He describes for us a meditation exercise which contains in its practice the seed to freeing us from our bondage and slavery to compulsive thoughts and emotions.

Roy's books are much more than an attempt to intellectually and verbally frame our common condition. He has purposed to use words so as to kindle a spark of wordless recognition in us that our lives have gotten out of our control.

As a psychologist of 30 years, I can assure the readers who approach Roy's books that they will find the key to the personal problems they confront. I have observed time and again the efficacy of Roy's teachings and practices in people of varying emotional maladies.

Ron Carlson PhD
Clinical Psychologist

What a pleasure and an honor it is to endorse this book!

I have had many years of training in the science of medicine. I have taught in universities and made contributions to medical literature and spent many years in private practice; then I heard Roy Masters' radio program. I must admit I was shocked at first, but I listened.

Although some of his statements appear contradictory to traditional scientific beliefs, I sensed an underlying ring of Truth. I was intrigued and sent for the literature.

I was astounded to find how right-on his principles were and how they filled in the gap I had always felt was missing in modern medicine. Today's fundamental misconception that science is the Truth is clearly rectified by what Roy Masters teaches.

The Foundation of Human Understanding has been a great help to me in my work with many difficult problem patients.

I must warn you, however, this book is not for everyone.

Albert R. MacKenzie, M.D .

"Right on target! Roy Masters revitalizes ageless wisdom. For many, one hour with Roy Masters will be more beneficial than years of traditional insight psychotherapy."

Clancy.D. MacKenzie
Director of Philadelphia
Psychiatric Consultation Service

The secret of life itself...

Resolve your fear, anger and guilt,
and discover your true identity.

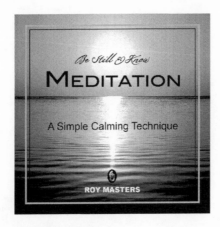

Most of us are the sum total of our experiences. Another way of saying this is that we are bothered, burdened, and sometimes disabled by our past. Unless we learn to respond correctly in the present moment, the present merely becomes an extension of the past that we are trying to leave behind.

Roy Masters teaches a simple observation/meditation exercise which enables the user to remain calm and patient in the face of extreme stress, confusion and cruelty. Based on Judeo-Christian roots, the exercise will help lead you back to your center of dignity and understanding and show you how to remain sane, poised and tranquil under the most severe trials and tribulations.

From Despair to
MEANING and HAPPINESS

You are the sum total of your experiences, but another way of saying this is that you are burdened by your past.

Take heart. . . there is not one single problem in the world that you cannot solve if you will understand the principle revealed in this extraordinary book—a principle that will help you uncover and neutralize the programming of your past.

Overcoming
Stress
Fear
& Pain

The key to dealing with stress, fear and pain is not as difficult to discover as it may seem. This series, based upon the technique found in the *Be Still and Know Meditation* exercise, will help you reconnect to the intuitive knowing in your heart, rather than responding to outside pressures.

BOOKS BY ROY MASTERS

HOW YOUR MIND WILL MAKE YOU WELL
The Foundation's best-selling primer on dealing with stress, emotional upset, and worry. Included are instructions on the Judeo-Christian meditation, that will help you to become objective to your thoughts and feelings. This objectivity will awaken in you a natural flow of understanding.

FROM DESPAIR TO MEANING & HAPPINESS
This book explains how our negative emotions are rooted in anger, fear, and guilt, and explains how to resolve the effects of trauma conditioning, and become the real "you" again.

THE SECRET POWER OF WORDS
What power do words have over you? Everyone has a sensitivity to words, whether those words are cruel or kind. This book explains how to break the spell.

UNDERSTANDING SEXUALITY
Why are women attracted to weak or abusive men? Why do people become homosexuals? What is the real reason for marital infidelity? Why do you feel guilty after sex? Find the answers in this fascinating book.

BEYOND THE KNOWN
Science has long claimed that people don't live up to their full potential. Those willing to break free from their past limitations will find a powerful assist in this insightful book.

EAT NO EVIL
What you are looking for in the refrigerator is in this book! *Eat No Evil* explains why diets don't work and reveals the psychology behind our fascination with food.

HYPNOTIC STATES OF AMERICANS
How is it that a stage hypnotist can take normal, well-educated people and quickly take control of their minds? In this book, Roy Masters reveals the mystery of early childhood conditioning, and how it leads people to react to hypnotic pressures and subtle suggestions in everyday life.

HOW TO SURVIVE YOUR PARENTS
The way you relate to your parents sets the pattern for all of the relationships in your life. This book shows how you can develop honest, positive relationships—both with your parents and with your children.

HOW TO CONQUER SUFFERING WITHOUT DOCTORS
"How much of your suffering—physical, psychological and emotional—has been

brought about by your own reactions to stress? More than you realize," says Roy Masters, and with this book he helps you to stop depending on others for your well-being.

SECRETS OF A PARALLEL UNIVERSE
Subtitled: Why Our Deepest Problems Hold the Keys to Ultimate Personal Success and Happiness. This book shows how a simple understanding of our conflicts, fears, and anxieties can lead directly to a recognition and appreciation of the way to true fulfillment.

THE ADAM AND EVE SINDROME
With the rate of divorce and family breakdown so high, how can a man or woman be assured of finding the right mate, or if already married, of avoiding the pain and suffering caused by marital failure? This book is a definitive guide to recognizing, understanding, and avoiding the mistakes that lead to broken hearts, homes, and health

GRAVITY DRIVEN UNIVERSE
In his newest book for laymen, philosophers and physicists, Roy Masters explores the mysteries of the cosmos, and explains how the universe was created. What you find here may well provide the keys to a new science for the 21st century.

SURVIVING THE COMFORT ZONE
Everyone runs away from pain into comfort of some kind. The problem is that when you get comfort, your problems still exist, and now you have yet another problem: you have become addicted to escaping.

OTHER MATERIALS
AVAILABLE FROM THE FHU

For over fifty years, Roy Masters and the Foundation of Human Understanding have been helping people to resolve their emotional, psychological and spiritual problems. The FHU has an extensive catalogue of literally hundreds of audio tapes, videos and books on subjects as diverse as man/woman relationships, raising children, sexuality, health, addiction, and religion.

For a complete catalogue of all the materials offered by the FHU:

Foundation of Human Understanding
PO Box 1000 • Grants Pass OR 97528, USA

1-800-877-3227 • www.fhu.com • books@fhu.com

Made in the USA
Charleston, SC
28 December 2011